# Detente: Promises and Pitfalls

# Detente: Promises and Pitfalls

GERALD L. STEIBEL

FOREWORD BY Irving Kristol

PUBLISHED BY

Crane, Russak &
Company, Inc.
NEW YORK

National Strategy
Information Center, Inc.

*Detente: Promises and Pitfalls*

*Published in the United States by*
Crane, Russak & Company, Inc.
347 Madison Avenue
New York, N.Y. 10017

Copyright © 1975 by
National Strategy Information Center, Inc.
111 East 58th Street
New York, N.Y. 10022

Library Edition: ISBN 0-8448-0660-9

Paperbound Edition: ISBN 0-8448-0661-7

LC 74-33205

Strategy Paper No. 25

*Printed in the United States of America*

# Table of Contents

# Preface

In July 1969, the National Strategy Information Center published a short monograph by Dr. Gerald L. Steibel on *Detente: Dilemma or Disaster?* At the time, the detente policy of the new Nixon Administration was just gathering momentum; and Dr. Steibel's study provided an early, critical examination of this controversial policy departure. Much has happened in the intervening six years. The SALT I and II negotiations with the Soviet Union have transformed the strategic arms race. East-West trade has grown substantially as a consequence of detente diplomacy; and in many other respects, our relations with the Soviet Union have been considerably modified.

It remains an open question, however, whether detente has yielded more benefits for American policy than debits. Many argue, for example, that we are worse off than ever before in the strategic arms race; that the transient benefits accruing to the United States from expanded trade with the Soviet Union hardly compensate for the high technology and other advantages we thereby transfer to the Soviet Union; and that there has been precious little pay-off in terms of liberalizing the Soviet regime.

The Vladivostok agreement of November 1974 on the strategic arms race, and Soviet cancellation in January 1975 of the US-Soviet trade agreement of 1972, were watershed developments in the long evolution of detente. They are especially interesting because they point in opposite directions. Together, they afford a convenient moment for summing up the whole experience of detente once more. In his new monograph, Dr. Steibel reviews the history of detente, with special reference to its impact on arms control, crisis management, economic relations, the putative "mellowing" of the Soviet regime, and relations with our European allies. His study is a kind of layman's guide to the subject, with careful emphasis on the pitfalls as well as promises of the detente process.

Dr. Steibel is at present Director of Foreign Affairs Research at the Research Institute of America. He has taught at Columbia, New York University, and the City University of New York. Formerly Research Director of the Free Europe Committee, Dr. Steibel has published numerous articles on problems of communism and international relations.

A recent essay by Irving Kristol of *The Wall Street Journal* on "The Politics of Appeasement" sets forth with striking clarity the dangers inherent in current efforts by the Congress to assert a dominant voice in the formulation of US foreign policy, and the prospect that this trend may lead to disastrous policies of appeasement in almost every quarter of the globe. His thoughtful analysis is reproduced with permission as a Foreword to Dr. Steibel's monograph on the opportunities and hazards of detente with the Soviet Union.

Frank R. Barnett, *President*
National Strategy Information Center, Inc.

March 1975

# Foreword

# THE POLITICS OF APPEASEMENT*

## Irving Kristol

We have, apparently, decided to rectify the transgressions of an imperial presidency by subjecting ourselves to the abuses of Congressional government. Though the former may have been more egregiously scandalous, the latter might well turn out to be more permanently destructive.

Most of the Presidential follies of the last six years had little to do with the presidency as such; they flowed quite simply from the character of Mr. Nixon and his close associates. In contrast, the follies that Congress will inflict on us have little to do with the persons of our incumbent Congressmen, who are presumably no worse or better, on average, than ever before. The abuses of Congressional government are fundamental to this kind of government itself, which is inevitably irresponsible government.

One forgets that the reason the Founding Fathers devised a constitution with a strong and independent President, constituting a separate branch of government, was because they had, in the previous decade, a most grievous experience with legislative dominance at both the national and state levels. This legislative dominance had resulted in the mismanagement of domestic affairs and impotence in foreign affairs. It always does have such effects. Congress, by its very nature, is incapable of taking the longer or larger view of any matter. As the ultimate organ of popular sovereignty, Congress is a creature of popular opinion, which it seeks to appease, never to refine or elevate. This intimate association with popular opinion is its source of strength in a constitutional crisis, but it is a source of weakness when it comes to the business of governing. To take a longer or larger or more comprehensive view of political matters means to defer gratifications, to impose temporary sacrifices, to make decisions about what the nation needs as distinct from what the people at any moment may unthinkingly desire. Not wishing to do such things, Congress is allergic to any perspective which might prescribe them.

### "The Social Pork Barrel"

This normal condition has been much aggravated, in recent years, by the development of what David Stockman calls "the social pork barrel." As the federal government has sponsored more and more programs which deliver goods and services for more and more people, each Congressman finds himself more firmly the captive of the particular constituency created by each program. His votes, then, become a series of discrete appeasements, and what they add up to he will not reckon. He really does believe that "What have you done for me lately?" is a legitimate—indeed, the crucial—question which the voters may properly put to him. And since he believes it, the voters naturally believe it, too.

Along with such irresponsibility in domestic (especially fiscal) affairs, there goes impotence in foreign policy. Precisely because Congress sees politics as the art of appeasing various constituences, it can never be serious about foreign policy, which consists in making one difficult and disagreeable and controversial choice after another. The truth is that Congress profoundly resents foreign policy matters, as rude intrusions in its quest for the popular, and wishes they would go away. Its instinct is to subordinate all matters of foreign policy to domestic (i.e., political) considerations. And it justifies this subordination with much wishful thinking and clouds of moralistic rhetoric.

The attitude of Congress toward President Ford's energy program is a case in point. It persists in focussing attention on the economic costs of this program, on the burdens it places on this or that part of the country, or on this or that sector of the population. What it resolutely overlooks is that *this is a foreign policy program*, not a domestic economic program at all. It is not a program to cope with an oil shortage (which does not now exist) or to cope with high oil prices (which it will not reduce). It is a program that has as its purpose the preservation of America's status as a world power, with the capability of conducting a foreign policy free from blackmail by the OPEC nations, as well as by any other group of nations that decides to form a cartel in one scarce commodity or another.

I do not suggest that President Ford's program is the best of all conceivable programs to achieve this purpose. There are other ways of accomplishing this end, and it is possible that one or another may be superior. But what is certain is that all of them will be costly, in the sense that they will represent a voluntary act of economic self-denial on the part of the American people in order to gain political freedom of action in international affairs. And it is predictable that Congress will conclude that such economic self-denial is unthinkable. It will not impose rationing; it will not impose import quotas; it will not even move to increase our oil production in the offshore Atlantic lest it inconvenience New Jersey's summer resorts. It will decide, rather, that we shall all be better off—i.e., more comfortable—with no kind of program at all.

In narrow and shortsighted economic terms, of course, such a decision has its own validity. There is no doubt that all Americans will be more comfortable without an act of self-denial than with it. Now that the sharp increase in energy costs has largely "passed through" the economy, and the initial painful adjustments have been made, it is even likely that if Congress does nothing, the economy will recover its natural equilibrium and proceed along a path of steady (if more modest) economic growth. Some economists think this is so—and some Republican politicians, seeing this possibility, even believe that such Congressional inaction will work to President Ford's advantage in 1976.

But this whole way of thinking about the matter ignores the point of an energy program, which is not to give something to the American people but to take something from them, so as to allow us and our allies to have a foreign policy we can call our own. Without some kind of energy program, American policy toward the Middle East will, in the event of a crisis and another oil embargo, or in the event simply of another sharp increase in oil prices, be limited to two alternatives: (a) immediate military intervention, or (b) abrupt appeasement. Though the former prospect has of late been speculated about, it remains academic for the while: after Vietnam, "intervention" is a dirty word. So appeasement will be the order of the day. As a matter of fact, it is clear that, by Congressional actions and inactions, appeasement is already the order of the day.

**Recalling the Past**

It is hardly an accident that Congress' refusal to devise an energy program coincides with an upsurge of speeches and articles and editorials about Israel which remarkably resemble those Anglo-French speeches and editorials about the Sudetenland and Danzig in 1938. Then, as now, small countries whose very existence was threatened by powerful neighbors were urged to be "reasonable"—i.e., to yield to the threat of force—in order to achieve "peace in our time." Then, as now, those doing such persuading promised ultimate support—but opposed an increased military budget because of the urgency of "unmet social needs." Then, as now, smaller and weaker allies were sold down the river so as to avoid the calamity of war. Then, as now, such appeasement only made war more probable, not less.

Though appeasement in the Middle East is now only beginning to take shape, it is already in full swing in Southeast Asia. One would have thought that, after our withdrawal from Vietnam, there could be no question of our moral obligation to provide the South Vietnamese with the miltary supplies needed for their self-defense. Instead, Congress has decided that the South Vietnam government is not "nice" enough to suit our liberal tastes, and that what happens there is in any case not of critical significance to our national interests. But if this is true of South Vietnam, why is it less true of South Korea, Malaysia, Singapore, Indonesia—or, in Europe, of Yugoslavia, Portugal, or Spain? None of these governments is a liberal democracy, in our sense of the term; and, in *isolation*, none of them is of great importance to us. But were they all to end up as members of an anti-American bloc, the shape of world politics would be decisively altered, and to our disadvantage. "Fortress America" might then become an ugly necessity, rather than a squalid fantasy.

It will be said by some that I am being bewitched by a version of the "domino theory," which equates the surrender of an inconveniently situated pawn or two with the loss of the entire chess game. The depreciation of the "domino theory" is always much favored by those who are set for appeasement. But in international politics, as in chess, the "domino theory" is usually more right than wrong. The Russians certainly take this theory seriously; they are not pouring arms into North Vietnam or Syria—or money into the Portuguese Communist Party—because of a primitive inability to read a map.

And, one wonders, what about Saudi Arabia itself? This antiquated and creaking despotism will surely, one of these days, be overthrown by a rebellion of young Arab nationalists, strongly anti-Western in outlook and hence anti-American. The very money it is now expending for its own economic development guarantees that eventuality. What shall we do then, if we have not devised an energy program that makes us and our allies less dependent on OPEC oil? Military action will be even less imaginable in those circumstances than it is now, since massive supplies of Russian (or Chinese) arms, along with "military technicians," will quickly pour into that country, and the threat of a Great Power confrontation would be proximate indeed. Moreover, the NATO countries, having witnessed the tranquil way we have "disburdened" ourselves of one small friendly nation after another, are not likely to have faith in any proposal we might then make. They will capitulate; Europe will become a Soviet "sphere of influence"; we shall be utterly isolated.

**The Nuclear Threat**

A farfetched scenario? Perhaps. But there is nothing farfetched in the prediction that, as we move down the ways of appeasement, those of our allies who still have a powerful yearning for national existence, and who have been relying on "the American umbrella," will quickly move to establish a nuclear "umbrella" of their own. South Korea already has taken steps to develop its own nuclear capability. Turkey, as a result of its experience at the hands of a mindless and petulant Congress, will follow suit. Pakistan has every intention of rendering itself less vulnerable to a nuclear India by making its own nuclear bombs. American appeasement means nuclear proliferation on a massive scale. And it is hard to see how much nuclear proliferation can, in the end, mean anything but nuclear devastation (or contamination) of a good part of the earth's surface—and possibly all of it.

This is the world we are in the process of bequeathing to our children, as Congress pecks away at the military budget, inflates spending on social programs, and sanctimoniously sheds one "troublesome" ally (as if there are any other kind!) after another. To those of us who have even the vaguest memories of the 1930s, it is all too chillingly reminiscent.

# 1

## The Pulse of Detente

Since the dawn of the nuclear age, the world's fears of holocaust
and its hopes for peace have turned on the relationship between
the United States and the Soviet Union . . . The destructiveness
of modern weapons defines the necessity of the task; deep differences in philosophy and interests between the United States
and the Soviet Union point up its difficulty . . . Paradox confuses
our perception of the problem of peaceful coexistence . . . The
challenge of our time is to reconcile the reality of competition
with the imperative of coexistence.[1]

With these words, Secretary of State Henry Kissinger launched his
long exposition of detente before the Senate Foreign Relations Committee on September 19, 1974. He had said everything in the statement many times before, but this was the first time he had brought
it all together in one formal presentation. It was a skillful job. There
was the rationale for detente, its evolution, a balancing of risks and
incentives, an agenda for the future. But what emerged, as the Secretary went through the 50 pages, was a brief, a plea, a set of warnings.
Detente is "continuing process, not a final condition;" we cannot
wait until there is "a convergence of American and Soviet purposes;"
we must not tie detente to "a basic change in Soviet motivation," or
use it "to produce internal changes in foreign countries."[2] And much
more.

---

[1] *Statement by the Honorable Henry A. Kissinger, Secretary of State, Before the Senate
Foreign Relations Committee,* September 19, 1974 (mimeographed), pp. 1, 2.
[2] *Ibid.,* p. 3.

Kissinger's detente was in trouble. A day earlier, arms limitation talks with the Soviet Union had resumed, but the United States did not even have a unified bargaining position as between the State and Defense Departments, and the prospect of an agreement with the USSR seemed slight. Trade relations with Russia were bogged down over the Jewish emigration issue, while Kissinger negotiated with Senators Jackson, Ribicoff, and Javits over tariff equality for Moscow. A month later, wheat sales to the USSR would be halted entirely. One of the few accomplishments of the June summit in Moscow, the ban on underground nuclear tests involving devices of more than 150,000 tons of TNT equivalent, was under such criticism in the United States that it could not be sent to the Senate for ratification.[3]

The atmosphere of detente was further clouded by news from the USSR. Soviet journals had unleashed a wave of cartoons attacking this country. One showed an evil-looking character labeled "CIA" oppressing the people of Chile. In another, Cambodian ruler Lon Nol was sitting in one hand of Uncle Sam and catching silver dollars from the other. There were caricatures of Israel as a Pentagon puppet, black students in Boston as victims of Ku Klux Klansmen, and so on in tones straight out of the coldest Cold War days.[4] Articles in the same publications denounced American scholars as agents of subversion. A number of leading US Sovietologists were being denied entry to the USSR. The publicity given to exiled author Alexander Solzhenitsyn's book, *The Gulag Archipelago*, it was made clear, was regarded as a hostile act.[5]

Something was wrong with detente, it seemed, but nobody was altogether sure where to pinpoint the problem. The respected *Economist* of London had expressed one general feeling about detente when it remarked of the June meeting that "it confuses confusable people in the West . . . (and) conceals how little thinking anybody has done . . . These are all negotiations that would have been handled better by the Western side if it had been clearer what detente means, and does not mean."[6] Three months later, the nature of the confusion,

---

[3] *Christian Science Monitor*, September 6, 1974.
[4] *New York Times*, September 25, 1974.
[5] *Ibid.*, September 22, 1974.
[6] *Economist*, June 29—July 5, 1974.

at least, was beginning to clarify. "No one is going to oppose the ideal of Soviet-American detente in its pure meaning," the *New York Times* said editorially, a week after Kissinger had made his exposition. "The issue is whether the pursuit of detente is being wisely conducted, with proper regard for fundamental interests and full realization of pitfalls as well as rewards."[7]

Few among the public at large would have quarreled with the editorial's first point. Detente was generally perceived as desirable and, in any case, inevitable. Scrapping it was not even in the mainstream of discussion, and no one appeared to have an alternative. Even AFL-CIO President George Meany, an outspoken critic of detente from the start, told the Foreign Relations Committee, "We're for a genuine detente," and spelled out the conditions: ending the Soviet ideological war, reversing the arms build-up, and freeing the flow of people and ideas in Eastern Europe and the USSR in return for American economic aid.[8]

The heart of the matter was the *Times*' second point: effective negotiation. "This country," the editorial warned, "may find itself settling for minimal tangible benefit for itself in pursuit of a desirable abstraction, while the Soviet leadership successfully extracts real concessions in return for empty lip-service." It complained that the "extent of the political cost which the Russians are willing to pay for this access (to US technology) has scarcely even been tested in American diplomacy." Finally, it cautioned, an "enthusiastic political leadership in the White House and State Department (fails to) insist that every single economic and political engagement with the Soviet Union be studied for its measure of mutual benefit, on its own terms."[9]

Sound as these injunctions are, they reveal something else that is missing in contemporary perceptions of detente—the historical dimension. There is a sense of surprise and dismay that this detente should be floundering. Historical memory often does not exceed three or four years, the life of the Nixon-Kissinger (and now Ford)

---

[7] *New York Times,* September 26, 1974.
[8] *Ibid.,* October 2, 1974.
[9] *Ibid.,* September 16, 1974.

policy. Kissinger himself refers in his statement only to the postwar years. But there is more to the tale than that. Detente did not begin in 1972, or 1969, or 1954 under Khrushchev. It goes back almost the entire course of the Soviet Union's history. For over half a century, American-Soviet detentes have been rising and falling. At least five such cycles are on the record—six, if the two phases of the present one are counted separately. Detente, the record reveals, is an idea whose time has come again and again, but never to stay. Each beginning has been greeted with enthusiasm, and each has been followed by disenchantment, only to lead after a time to another cycle.

It is time to raise and explore a series of questions about detente. What is the nature of this idea? What, as the *Economist* suggested, does it mean and not mean? How can it be studied clinically? Where and when did the process take root and grow, and why? And most of all, what does this history impart that may make it possible to deal with this and future detentes more effectively? A brief historical survey is the necessary starting-point.

1. *1920, The Lenin Detente.* With his world revolution a failure and his economy a shambles in the wake of World War, civil war, and the excesses of "war communism," Lenin turned to the West for help in 1920. That produced a $20 million credit from the Chase Bank in New York, $66.3 million in direct assistance from the US government, and the sale of seeds and foodstuffs to the Soviets for $10 million in gold.[10] In addition, American firms, among them the Ford Motor Company, sent between 600 and 700 engineers and technicians to help build dams, power stations, tractor plants, railroads and other heavy industry—all accompanied by a drumfire of Soviet propaganda against "bourgeois imperialism."[11]

This earliest detente brought a second and third feature of the process into existence: euphoria and disappointment. Lincoln Steffens went to Russia and made his classic announcement, "I have seen the future and it works"—apparently in contrast to the corruption Steffens had been exposing in American city government. British

---

[10] Albert L. Weeks, *The Other Side of Coexistence* (New York: Pitman, 1970), p. 99.
[11] *Ibid.*, p. 114.

historian H. G. Wells also made the journey, where he witnessed the Lenin terror. "Apart from individual atrocities," he wrote, "it did on the whole kill for a reason and for an end."[12] Wells was a gentle enough man. The heroes of his *Outline of History* are the teachers and lawgivers, and he had a Bergsonian faith in science as the vital force that was moving mankind toward a more civilized existence. Warriors and dictators received short shrift. Yet, like so many who would follow him, he could only see "ends" in Lenin's Russia, and rationalized means. Not everyone, it should be noted, shared Wells' view. John Dewey was repelled by the means. Summing up his experience in Russia in *Reason and Nature*, he argued that means become ends, and evil behavior can find no justification in any end.

In the event, the argument became academic when Lenin died and Stalin succeeded him. Detente faded as Stalin imposed the first Five-Year Plan (1928-33). American economic help continued to flow, but in much smaller volume. In Russia, Western ideas and contacts were reduced drastically; emphasis was on the collectivization of farms and the growth of capital industry; and Communist Parties throughout the world were sent into active struggle against established governments and societies.

2. *1935, Stalin's Detente.* Once again, the USSR called on the West when it was needed. This time, it was the Nazi threat to turn the Soviet lands into a "breadbasket" for Hitler's supermen, and the Soviet people into his slaves. Stalin ordered the Communist Parties in the West to join with democratic forces in socalled "popular fronts." The second detente was dogged from the start by Stalin's massive purges, which swept away whole segments of Soviet society, right up to the top. The popular front tactic did not generate the military security Stalin had hoped for from the West, but it did create a new surge of admiration for the Soviet "experiment."

As George Watson puts it, "the pro-Stalinist intellectual hysteria reached its climax in 1936-38."[13] Hewlett Johnson, the "Red Dean of Canterbury," wrote *The Socialist Sixth of the World* in 1939,

---

[12] George Watson, "Were the Intellectuals Duped?" *Encounter* (December 1973), p. 22.
[13] *Ibid.*

apparently oblivious to the forced labor camps. Beatrice and Sidney Webb did take note of the repressions, but like Wells contended that in Russia, "the greatese crime is that against the state," and called their book *Soviet Communism: A New Civilization.* Stephen Spender carried the Webb's argument further, writing that the repressive laws would someday be knocked away and political freedom eventually established.

The Stalin detente ended abruptly in August 1939, when he switched from the West to Nazi Germany. A few days after conclusion of the bilateral Nonaggression Pact, the Nazi invasion of Poland touched off World War II.

3. *1941, The Devil's Detente.* The author of the third detente was neither the USSR nor the West, but Adolf Hitler. As his armies crashed into Russia on June 22, 1941, Winston Churchill announced that he would ally with the Devil himself if that personage was fighting Hitler. American Lend-Lease aid flowed to the USSR in huge volume. Roosevelt, Churchill, and Stalin posed for pictures in a series of conferences on the war and its aftermath. Roosevelt referred to Stalin as "Uncle Joe over there in the Kremlin."

The Devil's detente hardly outlasted the war. In contrast to Western expectations of continued cooperation among the wartime partners, Stalin laid claim to hegemony in Eastern Europe, announced his designs on Turkey's Kars and Ardahan Provinces, and pursued a guerrilla war against Greece. Only the limited American military response in Greece, followed by a more general Western reaction in the establishment of the North Atlantic Treaty Organization after the Berlin blockade and airlift, in 1948-49, kept the situation from deteriorating further. By the time the final blow was delivered in the Korean War, in 1950, Stalin had converted the Yalta coalitions in Eastern Europe into virtual takeovers. The detente cycles had now taken on a new and more ominous note.

A new controversy arose over who was to blame. In 1952, Professor William Appleman Williams advanced the claim that the Cold

---

[14] Robert James Maddox, "Cold War Revisionism: Abusing History," *Freedom at Issue* (September—October 1972), pp. 3, 18, 19.

War had been instigated by the United States. American commitment to the Open Door policy, Williams contended, became in effect an American bid for global primacy. Soviet objectives, by contrast, were far more modest and defensive. Williams' contention has been taken up and amplified by a number of other revisionists. Gabriel Kolko's 1968 book, *The Politics of War*, argued that American wartime policy was to create "an integrated capitalism" after the war in which US power and influence would be paramount. Gar Alperovitz's *Atomic Diplomacy*, and David Horowitz's *The Free World Colossus*, interpret the Cold War as the consequence of President Truman's personal characteristics. Truman, in this view, destroyed the wartime partnership by dropping the atom bomb on Japan, not so much as a military act designed to end the war as a diplomatic move intended to intimidate the Russians in Eastern Europe and Asia.[14]

Professor Robert J. Maddox of Pennsylvania State University has studied the revisionists' evidence and conclusions. He says their assertions can be supported only by doing violence to the facts.[15] Pulitzer Prize-winning Professor Oscar Handlin of Harvard calls the revisionist thesis "inherently absurd . . . blandly disregarding everything we have learned from the other side," yet persuasive to a considerable bloc of opinion "because they supply a pseudo-historical basis for the wishful thinking of present-day isolationists."[16]

4. *1954, Khrushchev's Detente.* The fourth American-Soviet detente came out of a radically altered perception of the siutation on the part of both powers. On the Soviet side, a new leader was in Stalin's old seat, preaching "goulash communism" (consumer satisfactions, Western-style economic reform), denouncing Stalin's terror, and bent on getting Western help via "peaceful coexistence." On the American side, the failure of the 1953 uprisings in Eastern Europe and the introduction of nuclear arms in the powerful Soviet armies stationed there meant that Communist control was not only well entrenched but also a force to be reckoned with. For the first time, detente had become of necessity the framework for negotiation on something like a mutuality of power.

---

[15] *Ibid.*, p. 3.
[16] Oscar Handlin, "Revisionist History: A Base for Neo-Isolationism," *Freedom at Issue* (September—October 1972), p. 2.

Two meetings in Geneva launched the detente auspiciously. In 1954, the powers worked out a series of accords that was supposed to end the war in Indochina; and detente reached a high-water mark the next year with a summit meeting and the proclamation of the "Spirit of Geneva." The first sour note came as the 1955 conference was ending, with a Soviet announcement that it would begin shipping arms to Egyptian President Nasser. A year later, Nasser seized the Suez Canal, and open conflict with Britain, France, and Israel followed. Soviet-American detente bore immediate fruit for Khrushchev in what amounted to joint pressure on the Western allies to call off the fighting. A second dividend came at the same time in President Eisenhower's assurances during the Hungarian uprising that Soviet "legitimate interests" in Eastern Europe would not be challenged. Both events left Khrushchev secure in Eastern Europe and with an historically new foothold in the Middle East.

Khrushchevite detente entered its downside with a series of crises that were punctuated, however, with further expressions of amity and new negotiations. In 1957, the USSR sent up its first space vehicle, *Sputnik*, and demanded the Western powers get out of West Berlin. In 1959, Khrushchev visited the United States, toured Disneyland, and left with the impression that his "Spirit of Camp David" partner, President Eisenhower, was ready to meet his Berlin demand. When Khrushchev realized that Eisenhower had no such intention, and an American U-2 spy plane was shot down over Russia, he called off the summit meeting scheduled for 1960 in Paris, and staged his notorious shoe-banging performance at the United Nations. Soviet-American hostility rose to its most dangerous pitch yet in the Cuban missile crisis of late 1962, the first actual nuclear showdown between the two powers. The fourth detente was over.

Even as conflict deepened, the foundations for the next detente were being laid. Rising violence in Indochina threatened to involve the US and USSR in a direct confrontation. In 1962, an uneasy compromise was engineered among the warring factions in Laos that removed the immediate danger, but opened the way for expansion of the Soviet-backed "war of national liberation" in Vietnam. In 1963, the US and USSR concluded the Nuclear Test Ban Treaty, which halted testing in the atmosphere. Thus, the negotiating channels remained open for the next detente, as Khrushchev was replaced by Brezhnev and Kosygin in 1964.

5. *1968, Brezhnev's Detente—Phase One.* Two American decisions set the stage for the centerpiece, arms control. Both were based on Secretary of Defense McNamara's thesis that the United States had to take unilateral steps to halt its own nuclear arms development if arms negotiations were to succeed. One step was to hold the US missile force at 1,054 land-based intercontinental missiles (ICBM) and 656 submarine-launched missiles (SLBM)—in both of which categories the USSR was far behind. The other was to forego the deployment of an American ballistic missile defense (ABM)—a system which the USSR had already developed and made operational. The expectation was that the USSR would negotiate an arms control agreement based on a rough parity of nuclear weaponry. The second decision had to be reversed in 1967 and 1968 because the USSR refused to discuss any ban on ABM. Only after the US announced a go-ahead on ABM, in 1967, and Congress voted the appropriation in 1968, did the USSR agree to negotiate on arms control. On July 1, 1968, President Johnson called in the press, radio, and TV networks to say that US-USSR negotiations would begin. The negotiation detente had arrived.

The *Christian Science Monitor* expressed the general feeling of hopefulness. "The logic of events, the normal evolution of history, and the wishes of the world as a whole work for a gradual, long-term betterment between Russia and America." The *New York Times* was more cautious. "Detente—Shadow or Substance?" it asked editorially. Within seven weeks, part of the answer was forthcoming as Soviet troops were sent into Czechoslovakia to evict the Dubcek regime, whose backsliding threatened the whole Soviet position in Eastern Europe. A *Monitor* story on September 16 reported that the US Secretary of State had told the Soviet Ambassador that the United States would not intervene, but that detente would be "impaired." Senator Pell of Rhode Island called the Soviet invasion and the American response "a second Munich in Europe," for which the "illusory price of continued detente" was being paid. Despite these and similar expressions of disgust in the United States and Europe, the prevailing reaction was summed up by Professor Zbigniew

Brzezinski, a one-time advisor to President Johnson and Vice President Humphrey:[17]

> We must differentiate between our immediate outrage and our immediate retaliatory response to express this outrage, from our long-term policy of building bridges. In the short term, we should react, but in the long run we shouldn't flip.

6. *1972 Brezhnev's Detente—Phase Two.* The new Nixon Administration wasted little time on outrage or Soviet criminality. It began a round of arms control negotiations in 1969 that was to be the foundation of a much broader detente, embracing not only the full range of economic and cultural contacts with the Soviet Union, but the Chinese People's Republic as well. In February 1972, President Nixon went to Peking for a summit meeting with the Chinese Communist leaders; and three months later, he was in Moscow to formalize one of the most comprehensive and ambitious packages of agreements ever attempted by this country. In his report to Congress on June 1, he said: "This was the year when America helped to lead the world up out of the lowlands of constant war, and onto the high plateau of lasting peace."[18]

The 1972 detente package contained three basic compartments. First, there were ten formal agreements. An ABM treaty limited both powers to two ABM sites each, in effect leaving their respective populations hostage to a first strike by the other. A five-year interim agreement on offensive nuclear arms embodied affirmation of the Soviet lead in numbers of ICBMs and SLBMs, and in "throw-weight" —that is, warhead-power carrying capacity. A declaration on "Basic Principles of Mutual Relations" paired acceptance of Soviet "peaceful coexistence" with US emphasis on "moving from confrontation to negotiation." These agreements were followed by seven others covering trade, incidents at sea, science and technology, space, health, the environment, and cultural exchanges.

In the second compartment were five declarations of cooperative intent: Europe (Berlin, the Conference on Security and Cooperation,

---

[17] *New York Times*, August 25, 1968.
[18] Department of State, *Weekly Compilation of Presidential Documents*, vol. 8, no. 23 (June 5, 1972), p. 981. (Hereafter cited as *Presidential Documents*.)

the West German-Soviet treaty), the Middle East, Indochina (here, the differing approaches were noted), disarmament (including biological and chemical weapons), and strengthening the United Nations.[19]

Perhaps the most important provisions of the 1972 package were its unspoken assumptions, which formed the third compartment:

1. The Soviet lead in numbers of launchers and throw weight would be compensated by the US lead in numbers of warheads, which the USSR either could not or would not try to overcome. Henry Kissinger told a press conference: "There is a rough parity being maintained in terms of delivery vehicles. The Soviet Union has more megatonnage; we have more warheads."[20]

2. With rough parity assured, the USSR would now proceed toward a more durable curb on strategic and other arms systems. In fact, Kissinger said, "we have made it clear that the continuation of the defensive treaty depends importantly on there being a follow-on agreement on offensive weapons."[21]

3. Detente has become a process with a life of its own, whatever it does or does not produce. Speaking to the Soviet people on television, President Nixon said: "If we continue in the spirit of serious purpose that has marked our discussions this week, these agreements can start us on a new road of cooperation for the benefit of our people, for the benefit of all peoples."[22]

4. The nonmilitary agreements, particularly those on trade and cultural exchanges, would help to mitigate the rigors of Soviet rule over its own people, thus opening Europe to a greater two-way traffic over the "bridges," and making the USSR a less belligerent adversary. The question of Jewish emigration, Kissinger said, had come up in the negotiations, and Brezhnev was aware of the US position.

\*     \*     \*

---

[19] *Ibid.*, p. 934.
[20] *Ibid.*
[21] *Ibid.*, p. 940.
[22] *Ibid.*

This brief review suggests three conclusions about the nature and functioning of detente. First, detente is an up-and-down affair, not a straight-line evolution. "Every detente ends," as Allan Goodman puts it.[23] It is one of the pulses of international relations, and should be read on a variable, rather than a fixed, scale. Neither the euphoria nor the dismay at the rising and falling ends of the cycles, therefore, is really to the point.

Second, detente is an institutionalization of conflict, not a replacement for it. All of the Soviet leaders have stressed, as Brezhnev did in 1966, that peaceful coexistence does not apply to the "class and liberation struggles in the capitalist countries or in colonies."[24] Each detente has seen the renewal of conflict, both ideological and—in the last three—brink-of-war military. Detente is neither entente nor the prelude to entente. Detente is relaxation to permit conflict to continue on less dangerous levels. Entente is the abolition of conflict and the movement toward full amity and alliance. The distinction must be kept in mind if detente is to be handled effectively.

Third, detente has become a negotiating process. It is the climatic framework for a widening range of bargaining that has always included the transfer of economic, scientific, and technological resources from the West to the USSR. Since conflict is built into the framework, negotiation itself has become an expression of the adversary relationship. The Western peoples generally view negotiation as a good in itself, when in fact it is a neutral term whose merits and demerits are in the payoffs on the risks taken.

Thus, the bottom line of detente is the calculus of beneficial versus harmful results. The current detente has produced both. They need to be weighed one against the other, especially in the major areas of the arms race, crisis management in the Middle East, trade, and internal Soviet repression, as well as the collateral effects on America's alliances—all of which have agitated discussion in the West since the 1972 package was adopted.

---

[23] Allan Goodman, "Every Detente Ends," *Freedom at Issue* (March—April 1974), pp. 3-5.
[24] L. I. Brezhnev, "Report of the Central Committee of the CPSU to the 23d Congress of the CPSU." *Moscow News*, April 2, 1966, p. 15.

Detente, obviously, is unfinished business. It responds faithfully to changing conditions, and both aims and tactics change accordingly. There is no inevitable outcome. Either lasting peace or nuclear holocaust, or any of the permutations in between, could ensue. To study detente in 1974, therefore, is to try to keep up with a rapid and still-unpredictable evolution. Nevertheless, a cutoff point after "Summit Four"—the December meetings in Vladivostok—is a convenient and reasonable time for beginning the much-needed audit.

# 2

## Arms and Detente

Arms control is the core of Soviet-American detente in the 1970s, the make-or-break factor that overrides every other negotiating area. The detente can promise a variety of agreements in trade, science, health, and cultural exchange; but its overall viability depends on curbing or reversing the deadly and expensive arms race that brought the two countries to the bargaining table in the first place. As Nixon and Brezhnev stated jointly in the preamble to the ABM Treaty, their aim was "to achieve at the earliest possible date the cessation of the arms race and to take effective measures toward reductions in strategic arms, nuclear disarmament, and general and complete disarmament."[1] Premier Kosygin said of the agreements that it "has become possible only on the basis of strict observance of the principle of equal security of the sides and the inadmissability of any unilateral advantages."[2] Ambassador Gerard Smith, the chief US negotiator, echoed these sentiments, saying that one should not ask "Who won?" and that "the future will record that both sides won."[3]

The 1972 arms pacts thus defined their own test, against which they are to be judged: first, the two countries must assure that the negotiations continue; and second, a more permanent arms control system guaranteeing something called "equality" must be attained. Two years after these tests were established, and six years after the negotiations had begun in 1968, the first of them had been met. As Alastair Buchan, former head of the British Royal College of Defense

---

[1] *Presidential Documents*, p. 925.
[2] *Ibid.*, p. 924
[3] *Ibid.*, p. 930.

Studies, remarked to an interviewer, the negotiations had "kept the momentum of Soviet-American dialogue going."[4] Furthermore, agreements had been produced, the scope of the negotiations widened, and both parties understood each other's capabilities and intentions better, reducing the chances of an outbreak of war through miscalculation.

The ultimate test of the arms negotiations, however, is not how well they perpetuate themselves but what they produce or fail to produce. In the view of one former US arms negotiations advisor, Professor William Van Cleave, Americans have been overly-fascinated with the process, thereby getting stuck with a bad product. They have tended to look at the negotiations as "talks" whose outcome was predetermined, and therefore "approached and conducted as if they were a kind of seminar where basic truths would be discussed and agreed upon, after which things would fall into place, not as a result of the bargaining process, but almost automatically as a result of analysis and logic."[5] Such an approach, Van Cleave contends, led the United States to retreat from its 1969 objectives, finally accepting agreements in 1972 that would have been considered unacceptable earlier.[6]

Whatever the merits of these particular judgments their emphasis on substance rather than process is necessary in order to weigh the product in the only terms that matter—cold national interest and security. In this vein, the magazine *National Review* urged: "The 'Spirit of Detente' would seem to have been sufficiently celebrated . . . the problems of detente are now, or should be made to be, specific: just what quids for our quos?"[7] The arms negotiations, properly analyzed, are a page in the ledger of detente. Each agreement made or unmade is a credit or debit to one or the other side, and that is where judgment should be rendered. To be specific:

1. *The Anti-Ballistic Missile Treaty* is generally regarded as relatively the most satisfactory for both sides, the nearest thing to the "no advantage" desideratum set up by mutual consent as the aim of

---

[4] *US News and World Report*, July 15, 1974, p. 16.
[5] US Senate Subcommittee on National Security and International Operations, Committee on Government Operations, *Hearings*. July 25, 1972, p. 201. (Hereafter cited as *Senate Hearings*.)
[6] *Ibid.*, p. 210.
[7] *National Review*, July 19, 1974, p. 794.

all the arms negotiations. The 1972 Treaty, which limited ABM sites to two for each side, and the 1974 Protocol, which reduced the number to a single site, met the desires of both countries to avoid an extensive ABM investment. The absence of defenses against second-strike retaliatory blows presumably reduces the incentives to mount first-strike attacks, thus helping to stablize relations and promote further control measures, as well as cutting expenditures. Hence, the ABM Treaty appears as a rough model of "non-zero-sum" negotiation (that is, where no winner takes all), and meets what had been the US aspiration prior to Secretary McNamara's reluctant decision in 1967 to proceed with a US ABM.

On the other side of the ledger, there are certain considerations that need to be taken into account. One showed through briefly in Kissinger's news conference of May 26, 1972, when he remarked: "It is perhaps true that in the ABM field we had the more dynamic program, which is being arrested as a result of these developments."[8] This remark helps explain at least one reason why the USSR was willing to conclude the ABM Treaty. Van Cleave is much more direct. After reviewing the initial US determination to obtain ABM-ICBM limitations that would safeguard US missile strength *vis-à-vis* Soviet capabilities, he asserts that the ABM-ICBM "match" was lost. As a consequence, "If ABM is to be limited as stipulated by the Treaty, the offensive capability permitted the Soviet Union is intolerable."[9]

The wisdom of limiting ABM defenses has come under a different kind of attack by Donald Brennan of the Hudson Institute, who argues that ABMs should be expanded rather than eliminated. In an April 1969 article, Brennan cited figures by Secretary of Defense McNamara indicating that ballistic missile defense systems costing from $10 to $20 billion could reduce American fatalities in a war to between 10 and 40 million, with similar reductions in property damage. He concludes:[10]

Thus, such a defense might change the postwar situation from one in which over half the US population was gone, and recov-

[8] *Presidential Documents*, p. 930.
[9] *Senate Hearings*, p. 233.
[10] D. G. Brennan, "The Case for Missile Defense," *Foreign Affairs* (April 1969), p. 434.

ery in any time period would be problematical, to one in which perhaps 90 percent survived and economic recovery might be achieved in five to ten years. This difference would be enormous.

It is this possible difference that constitutes the major reason for deploying heavy defenses. In effect, procuring such defenses is like buying "insurance" that would limit the consequences of a war; the outcome would still be a disaster, but probably one of a very different order than would result from having the same offensive force expended in a war with no missile defense.

To pursue deterrence via offensive weapons, Brennan further contends, is not only wrong but delusory. "Assured destruction" of 50 million Russians and half of Russia's industrial capacity by these weapons is far from "assured," and by inviting the USSR to strengthen its own offensive weapons, the concept leads to an American "assured vulnerability."[11] What Brennan is saying amounts to this: Both countries should be encouraged to move toward a mutual buttoning-up of defenses, seeking to make them so effective that reliance on offensive weapons will become obsolete.

Brennan's arguments have not prevailed, of course; but it is worth noting that official US uneasiness with the principle of making mass populations hostage to deterrence has persisted. One outgrowth has been Secretary Schlesinger's program to retarget the US missile forces away from population centers and onto military facilities.

2. *The Nuclear Test Ban* extension to underground explosions is similarly perceived as "useful" and likely to slow the growth of warheads, to quote Buchan again.[12] In fact, the ban contains so many questionable provisions that the Administration could not send the agreement to the Senate for ratification because of the opposition it had provoked.

Objections centered on two provisions. The first was Article I, which allows underground nuclear testing up to 150 kilotons yield[13]—

---

[11] *Ibid.,* p. 440.
[12] *US News and World Report,* July 15, 1974, p. 16.
[13] *New York Times,* July 4, 1974.

about seven times the power of the Hiroshima bomb. At a news conference on July 25, 1974, scientists from the Federation of American Scientists and Arms Control Association asserted that Soviet compliance with the "threshold" limit could not be verified. Herbert Scoville, Jr., former CIA and Arms Control and Disarmament Agency science and technology chief, said: "This is such an obvious loophole I don't know how the negotiators missed it." Russia could detonate 300 kiloton shots and call them 150 kiloton, and no one would know the difference, he added.[14] A State Department official replied that the US did have ways of checking, but Scoville was unconvinced.[15] Two other scientists, G. W. Rathjens and J. P. Ruina, of the Massachusetts Institute of Technology, wrote: "There would be no effect on the new Soviet missile programs, since it is inconceivable that the Soviet Union would conclude such an agreement without already having tested suitable warheads for these missiles."[16] Secretary Schlesinger was quoted as saying that no US weapon currently being tested would be affected.[17]

The second objection was to Article II, which excludes from the ban "underground nuclear explosions carried out by the parties for peaceful purposes"—such explosions to be negotiated in the future.[18] State Department negotiators defended this provision as an initial step toward bringing all explosions under negotiation; but the scientists argued that meanwhile "peaceful" explosions could not be distinguished from nonpeaceful. In August 1974, the Federation issued a statement denouncing the treaty as "worse than nothing," giving both countries a license to go on with nuclear weapons development.[19]

Much more than arms testing is at stake in these controversies, including nuclear energy for economic development, for example. Russia has used nuclear power to change the course of rivers. The US "Plowshare" operation is designed to extract new energy from sources deep underground. India has similar plans. But what is most at stake is whether or not detente can safely separate productive

---

[14] "Critics See Verification Problem." *Science*, August 9, 1974, p. 507.
[15] *Ibid.*
[16] G. W. Rathjens and J. P. Ruina, "Should We Ban Nuclear Testing Now?" *Science*, July 5, 1974, p. 5.
[17] *US News and World Report*, July 15, 1974.
[18] *New York Times*, July 4, 1974.
[19] *Christian Science Monitor*, September 6, 1974.

uses of nuclear explosions from destructive ones. By challenging Soviet good faith, the scientists have raised the question whether any ban on weapons testing can be trusted, short of the onsite inspection that the USSR adamantly rejects. The scientists have also spotlighted the tactical problem of whether to accept these first, admittedly inadequate, steps as a move toward a full and workable ban, or to insist on the whole package as the only objective.

3. *The Five-Year Interim Agreement on Offensive Missiles* has generated some of the sharpest attacks, as well as provocative justifications. To begin with, Senator Jackson has pointed out the basic fact of the Interim Agreement:[20]

> When SALT I began in late 1969, the United States had 1,054 land-based ICBMs and 41 Polaris-type submarines. The Soviets then had about 1,050 land-based ICBMs and no Polaris-type submarines. When the Interim Agreement expires on July 1, 1977, we will still have our 1,054 ICBMs and our 41 Polaris submarines. But the Soviets, depending on how they exercise their options, will have from 1,400 to 1,618 ICBMs and 62 Polaris-type submarines. The agreement confers on the Soviets a 3-to-2 advantage in numbers of land- and sea-based launchers, and a 4-to-1 advantage in throw-weight. In other words, in less than ten years, the world's strategic balance will shift dramatically; this shift is what has been codified in the SALT I accords.

Jackson goes on to outline the possible threats, political as well as military, as the Soviet Union exploits this strategic advantage in the future.

These charges have been met in two ways. The official US position was stated by Kissinger on May 27, 1972, when he revealed that the USSR was building ICBMs at the rate of 250 a year and SLBMs at the rate of 128 a year. "So this is the backdrop against which you have to assess the agreement." Since the United States had no ongoing building programs in either field, it faced "a numerical margin

---

[20] Henry M. Jackson, "We Must Not Mismanage SALT II," *Freedom at Issue* (May—June 1973), p. 2.

that was growing, and a margin, moreover, which we could do nothing to reverse in (the next) five-year period . . . The question is, What would this margin have been without the freeze? That is the justification for the margin."[21] This is an argument from necessity, and it may be persuasive as far as it goes. We did the best we could with what we found when we arrived; the alternative would have been worse. Implied in the argument, however, is the thesis that something had gone awry in the past, saddling this Administration with the necessity of making the best of a bad situation. The arms negotiations as a whole, in short, had serious deficiencies, by Kissinger's own telling.

An altogether different kind of defense is made on the nongovernmental level, typical of which is that put forth in the *Defense Monitor*, the publication of the Center for Defense Information. The Center is directed by retired US Admiral Gene R. LaRocque, who has been consistently critical of US arms policies. Explaining the 1972 Interim Agreement, the *Defense Monitor* wrote that the USSR was "years behind in MIRV, (while) the Soviet Union was increasing numbers of missile launchers and deploying larger vehicles to carry fewer warheads." While pointing out that the USSR could go on to build MIRVs, the *Defense Monitor* concludes:[22]

> Broadly speaking, the accords accommodate themselves to the different kinds of offensive weapons build-up which each side has underway now—Soviet construction of more and bigger missiles and US MIRV. They allow each to substantially complete the round it now has in progress. The new levels become the starting point for attempting to freeze the arms race.

The implication of this interpretation is unspoken, but altogether clear: SALT I has traded off Soviet advantages with US advantages— launcher numbers and megatonnage versus warhead numbers. Since neither side can, or intends to, overtake the other, the time is ripe for a weapons freeze, to be followed by arms reductions, budget cuts, and so on. The *Defense Monitor* thesis is a classic justification of the negotiating process, as it has functioned in the strategic arms

---

[21] *Presidential Documents*, p. 932.
[22] *Defense Monitor* (July 1972) pp. 2, 3.

area. If sustained by the facts, the thesis would have signalled a dramatic breakthrough for detente, opening the way to a genuine and lasting stability.

It did not take long for the flaw in the thesis to emerge. By the fall of 1973, US intelligence was reporting new Russian silos evidently intended to house another generation of missiles. In February 1974, four test-firings of those missiles were detected. Three of the new systems were MIRV carriers. The true impact of the 1972 Interim Agreement now was clear. With the nearly 2,600 launchers and an estimated 10 to 12 million tons of power[23] protected by the Agreement, the USSR could, if it decided, put something like 17,000 warheads into the skies,[24] enough to threaten the entire US land-based missile force. Against that, the U.S. could field about 2 million tons of power in 10,000 warheads.

The United States tried to rectify this potential imbalance at the 1974 Moscow Summit, but failed. American proposals to limit MIRV deployment on both sides were met with Soviet demands for continuation of its lead in missile numbers, parity in warheads, prohibition of new US submarine and bomber plane construction, and inclusion of US nuclear forces in Europe in the allowable levels of American strength.[25] The United States rejected the proposal, and the meeting ended without the follow-up pact envisaged in 1972. Kissinger complained publicly about the generals and admirals, saying that the US and USSR "have to convince their military establishments of the benefits of restraint, and that is not a thought that comes naturally to military people on either side."[26] In a news conference later the same day, Secretary Schlesinger said in rebuttal: "I think we have firm civilian control."[27]

Six months later, a nuclear arms agreement was reached at Vladivostok, but its provisions only deepened the questioning and controversies over the direction SALT was taking. Kissinger and Ford left no doubt that this was the follow-up agreement that the US had been

[23] *New York Times,* May 29, 1974.
[24] *Ibid.,* July 5, 1974.
[25] *Ibid.,* July 9, 1974.
[26] James Reston in *ibid.,* July 10, 1974.
[27] *Ibid.,* July 4, 1974.

seeking since 1972. Kissinger announced at a press conference in Vladivostok, as the meeting came to an end on November 24, that the agreement "marks the breakthrough with the SALT negotiations that we have sought to achieve in recent years," and forecast a comprehensive treaty in 1975 that would govern nuclear armaments for the next ten years.[28] Ford remarked that a "good agreement that will serve the interests of the United States and the Soviet Union is within our grasp."[29]

On December 2, Ford went on television and revealed the details of the agreement, which he said "puts a cap on the arms race." The formula placed a ceiling on numbers of launchers—2,400 land- and sea-based long-range missiles and heavy bomber planes. Of the missiles, 1,380 might be fitted with multiple warheads.[30] When Kissinger again met the press, on December 7, the first question was about "throw-weight," which was by omission still heavily in Soviet favor. Kissinger replied that throw-weight was not the issue and repeated his description of a "breakthrough," but now pinned his reasoning to the same argument he had used to defend the 1972 agreement—"if one compares the numbers not with some hypothetical model that one might have in mind, but with what would have happened in the absence of this agreement."[31]

Meanwhile, Secretary of Defense Schlesinger was airing his own assessment of the agreement. In carefully chosen words, he praised it as "a diplomatic achievement for the President" and as "a diplomatic breakthrough." He approved the "equality" written into the pact, and professed no deep concern with "balance." But "stability" was something else. "To improve technologies or to improve deployments tends to stabilize the arms race . . . technologies will continue to change, and we will continue to make adjustments." Did this mean that the arms race would now shift from "quantity" to "quality?" Schlesinger preferred not to call this a "qualitative arms race;" but he made it entirely clear that the only reason the agreement was

[28] State Department Release No. 511, "Kissinger Press Conference at Vladivostok," November 24, 1971, p. 1.
[29] Associated Press dispatch, Washington, D.C., November 25, 1974, in *New York Post*.
[30] *New York Times*, December 3, 1974.
[31] State Department Release No. 518, December 7, 1974, pp. 5-6.

acceptable was that it left the United States free to match or out-pace the USSR in weapons sophistication and effectiveness.[32]

What these issues were all about was summed up with evident dismay by the *New York Times* in an editorial on December 18:

> The Vladivostok agreement would permit the Soviet Union, starting next year, to replace with new, bigger, more accurate MIRV-tipped rockets virtually all the ICBMs it is permitted under the 1972 SALT I accords—1,380 of its 1,410 silo-based missiles. Before 1985, its present 1,410 warheads would go to an estimated 6,700. With their large size, this is more than *three times* the number of warheads needed for a "high-confidence" strike at the United States' 1,054 ICBM silos.

The editorial recalled that the March and June 1974 negotiations with the Russians were supposed to head off exactly that possibility. "For reasons that are still unclear—and which the Congress should urgently probe—that approach was abandoned by President Ford at Vladivostok, if not before." In words that could have been used by Secretary Schlesinger, with whom the *Times* does not often agree, the editorial said: "Crisis instability—the penultimate danger of the nuclear era . . . clearly has been brought closer by the failure at Vladivostok to limit MIRV missiles to low levels."[33]

A Harris Poll in December reflected the same disquiet in the public at large. The concept of a numbers limit was popular, but only a narrow plurality, 35 to 34 percent, believed that Vladivostok was "a major breakthrough." By 47 to 17 percent, moreover, Americans say there will be substantial continuation of the arms race; and 46 to 27 percent think that the Russians are unlikely to keep their end of the bargain.[34]

4. *Reciprocal Reduction of Armed Forces and Armaments* in Europe and elsewhere ranked close behind the strategic arms ob-

---

[32] "News Conference With Secretary of Defense Schlesinger" (mimeo, no source), December 6, 1974, p. 7.
[33] *New York Times* editorial, "Gaps at Vladivostok," December 18, 1974.
[34] *New York Post*, December 23, 1974.

jectives of the 1972 accords. The term "reciprocal," to the United States and its NATO allies, meant "mutual and balanced force reductions" (MBFR), "balanced" signifying larger Soviet than US reductions because of the USSR's greater numbers and closer geographical proximity. To the USSR, "balanced" had no place; it refers to "mutual reduction of forces and armaments and associated measures in Central Europe"—MURFAAMCE—which marks its own, and far different, interpretation of what the detente is expected to yield in this area.

The differing expectations showed up most clearly in the jousting over troop cuts in Europe, where NATO has 770,000 men, of whom 190,000 are American, and the Warsaw Pact has 900,000, half of them Soviet. According to the London *Economist*, NATO's MBFR proposal would impose cuts that would bring both sides to 700,000; the Warsaw Pact's MURFAAMCE would reduce NATO's forces to 641,250 and the Pact's to 752,000.[35] Soviet troops in Hungary would not be included in any pullback. As in the nuclear weapons negotiations, troop cuts could not get by Soviet determination to keep its lead. At the end of 1974, the impasse showed no signs of being broken.

If nothing more than troop numbers and ratios were at stake, the Soviet bargaining position might not reflect too unfavorably on the detente spirit. Holding out for advantageous terms is part of the negotiating process, and is generally not considered too disturbing. But when the rest of the structure is examined—the "armaments and associated measures"—a more somber light is cast. For example:[36]

—Soviet Frog and Scud surface-to-surface missiles in Europe have increased by 25 percent, helping to bring Russian nuclear munition stocks to the 7,000 level of US-NATO forces.

—Soviet T-62 tanks—the most modern—have risen from 5,040 to 6,500 among Soviet forces in East Germany. The USSR

---

[35] *Economist*, December 22, 1973.
[36] Drew Middleton in *New York Times*, July 1, 1974.

and its Warsaw Pact allies now have 19,000 tanks, against NATO's 6,700.

—Armored personnel carriers have increased by 4,000 vehicles since 1968.

—New 7-ton trucks have been introduced, heavy folding bridges have been provided, and river-crossing and commando units have been reequipped and reinforced.

Behind these efforts is what two Rockefeller University specialists, Frederick Seitz and Rodney Nichols, call "the extraordinary Soviet investment in R&D over the last decade." As a result, they say, "our technological leadership is eroding fast," as "Congress tends to be skeptical about longer-range R&D." Both the Defense Department and Congress underestimate and underfund prototype testing, thus imperiling "the one crucial capability that the US still possesses."[37]

It is arguable, of course, to what extent the survival of the United States is imperiled by these Soviet build-ups in arms. Secretary of Defense James Schlesinger, for example, has said that the USSR does not as of now have a strategic advantage, although he added that the US task was to prevent that from happening.[38] He also wrote in his 1975 *Report* that the Soviet Union "has historically been a relatively sober power, and I trust it will continue to be so."[39] Others have contended that US power is so enormous that the country cannot be overcome, regardless of how the SALT or troop-arms negotiations go. From the more specific standpoint of detente, however, these arguments are beside the point. In terms of arms control, the detente was expected both to promote numerical parities and to relieve the United States of dependence upon ultimate threats of holocaust. Thus far (year-end 1974), that expectation remains to be fulfilled.

---

[37] Frederick Seitz and Rodney W. Nichols, *Research and Development and the Pospects for International Security* (New York: Crane, Russak & Company, 1973), pp. 44, 45. Seitz is President, and Nichols Vice President, of Rockefeller University.
[38] *US News and World Report*, May 13, 1974, p. 39.
[39] US Department of Defense, *Annual Report*, FY 1975, p. 3.

# 3

## Crisis Management

Close behind the control of arms, on the detente agenda, is the control of crises, especially in the Middle East. The brink-of-war confrontation in the 1970 Jordan-Syrian crisis was fresh in the minds of the leaders of both superpowers when they met in Moscow in 1972. "The two sides," their informal agreement read, ". . . reaffirm their support for a peaceful settlement in the Middle East in accordance with Security Council Resolution 242." Such a settlement, the communique went on, "would open prospects for the normalization of the Middle East situation and would permit, in particular, consideration of further steps to bring about a military relaxation in that area."[1]

"Normalization" is a favorite Soviet word, developed in the Berlin crises and implying acceptance of Soviet conditions for settlement. Elaborating on the negotiations that produced the agreement, Secretary Kissinger put them in the "frank and thorough" category mentioned in the general introduction to the 1972 agreements—thereby implying that there had been considerable friction in the discussions. Nonetheless, he said, the Middle East announcement belonged in the area where there were prospects for greater cooperation, rather than continuing difference. "Both sides favor progress toward a peaceful settlement,"[2] he added; and Nixon and Brezhnev reaffirmed this when the latter came to Washington for the June 1973 Summit.

---

[1] *Presidential Documents*, p. 949. This declaration was reconfirmed when Brezhnev and Nixon met in Washington in November 1973.
[2] *Ibid.*, p. 951.

None but the most naive—of whom there were few—expected these carefully-hedged sentiments to eliminate the Middle East as a source of Soviet-American rivalry. What the United States did expect, as subsequent events demonstrated, was Soviet adherence to at least three ground rules: first, the USSR would try to influence its Arab friends not to bring on another Middle Eastern war; second, if another war did threaten, the Russians would let the Americans know about it before its outbreak; and third, if war did break out, the USSR would collaborate with the United States to contain and end it.

In sum, as Walter Laqueur later observed, to the Washington government, it was "unthinkable for the Russians to allow a situation to arise—let alone deliberately foment it—which would jeopardize all the progress that had been made during the past two years in US-Soviet relations."[3] Laqueur continues:

> These comforting beliefs collapsed within a few hours on October 6, 1973, not because of an intelligence failure or some tactical miscalculation, but because it had become the fashion in Washington to attribute aims to Soviet detente policy which were apparently quite unreal. Though many American policy-makers dimly realized that their concepts of detente and peaceful coexistence were not quite identical with Soviet views about these subjects, they were not aware of the extent of the differences.

Laqueur points out that the USSR had some 4,000 military advisors in Egypt and Syria at the outbreak of war, who could hardly have failed to see the preparations. Egyptian President Sadat, moreover, consulted with Brezhnev two weeks before the war began; and at the very least, Brezhnev seems to have raised no objections.

Laqueur's thesis was supported by *New York Times* correspondent Tad Szulc at a later date, when more evidence was available. Kissinger, busily discussing peace plans and "lulled into this false sense of security," was unaware that "Moscow had provided the Egyptians

---

[3] Walter Laqueur, "Detente: What's Left of It?" *New York Times Magazine*, December 16, 1973.

with lethal antitank Sagger missiles and SAM-6 antiaircraft missiles that were to take a terrible toll of Israeli tanks and planes."[4] More-over, according to two CBS correspondents, Bernard and Marvin Kalb, the spell of detente lasted well into the first stage of the fight-ing. As they reconstruct the rush of events, Nixon's and Kissinger's first reaction to the outbreak of hostilities on October 6, 1973, was to urge "restraint" on Egypt and Israel. Kissinger was particularly in-sistent with Israel's Foreign Minister, Abba Eban, whom he told, "Don't preempt." At the same time, Kissinger called on Soviet Ambassador Dobrynin for help in containing the crisis. Dobrynin said he would try. Throughout that first day, the Kalbs report, Kissinger continued to bring heavy pressure to bear on Israel not to take the military offensive. The Meir Cabinet went along, against the strong pleading of Israeli Chief of Staff Elazar. Mrs. Meir had several reasons for her decision—costs, the Yom Kippur holiday, con-fidence in Israel's fighting capacities, and so forth. But in the Kalbs' view, or perhaps most important, she didn't want to go against Kissinger's injunctions."[5]

The massive Arab attack across the Suez Canal that cracked Israel's defenses shook Kissinger's belief in the detente as a stabilizing factor, but did not quite eradicate it. The top-level Washington Special Action Group (WASAG) ordered four US warships to move from Athens to Crete as a precautionary step, but Kissinger con-tinued to hold back on material help to Israel. "He did not want to be provocative . . . to antagonize the Russians or the Arabs."[6] By October 8, American help had begun to flow toward Israel, and Kissinger warned that "detente cannot survive irresponsibility in any area, including the Middle East." The next day, reports came in citing a large Soviet sealift going toward Egyptian and Syrian ports, and a rise in the number of Soviet warships in the Mediterranean. Brezhnev sent a message to Algerian President Boumedienne urging the Algerian people to "use all means at their disposal and take all the required steps with a view to supporting Syria and Egypt in the difficult struggle imposed by the Israeli aggressors."[7]

[4] Tad Szulc, "Is He Indispensable? Answers to the Kissinger Riddle." *New York Times*, July 1, 1974.
[5] Marvin Kalb and Bernard Kalb, "Twenty Days in October." *New York Times Magazine*, June 23, 1974.
[6] *Ibid.*
[7] *Ibid.*

What really changed Kissinger's attitude was the report on October 10 of a Soviet airlift into Damascus and Cairo, involving the USSR's largest transport plane, the Antonov-22. That was followed by another report to the effect that three Soviet airborne divisions in Eastern Europe had been placed on alert. The Arab-Israeli crisis was rapidly becoming a US-USSR showdown, "a murderously dangerous situation, much worse, much more dangerous than the 1970 Jordan crisis," in Kissinger's own words. He now decided, the Kalbs say, that Russia had to be stopped, not only to save Israel, but to head off a much greater confrontation, to "create a new reality."[8] Detente, for the time being, was nowhere to be seen. As in Berlin, Korea, Vietnam, and the Middle East in 1970, the "new reality" was the application of raw American power, via Israel and more directly.

It took effect quickly, as American C-5s "rumbled into Tel Aviv, each one a signal of US determination." Israeli troops, replenished with US material, drove back across the Suez Canal. Now it was Egypt's turn to ask for help. On October 16, Premier Kosygin flew into Cairo with a cease-fire plan, promising President Sadat that Russia would enforce it alone, if necessary. The extreme terms of the cease-fire—Israeli withdrawal from all Arab lands—brought Kissinger to Moscow on October 20.[9] There, he learned that Saudi Arabia, the largest of the Arab oil-producing countries and purportedly an American "friend," had joined the embargo against shipments to the West.

There seems little doubt that the initiative for the oil embargo came from the Arabs themselves. Emotions against Israel were running high; and besides, the oil producers saw their chance to raise prices to exorbitant levels. But if the Soviet Union had little or nothing to do with the imposition of the embargo, it had much more to do with its length. Victor Zorza, a long-time specialist in Soviet affairs, reported in March 1974, that "had it not been for Moscow, the embargo might have been lifted long ago . . . the decision about the lifting of the embargo is tied to the question of an Arab-Israeli settlement, and the Soviet Union has been in a position to delay a

---

[8] *Ibid.*
[9] *Ibid.*

settlement and thus the lifting of the embargo." Zorza cites repeated Soviet broadcasts urging the Arabs to continue the ban on shipments, warning over and over that the United States was engineering a sell-out to Israel. The purpose was not to obtain a better settlement for the Arabs, but to "keep the Arabs and the United States at daggers drawn" and thus serve more basic Soviet aims.[10]

The October 20 negotiations with Brezhnev produced a United Nations Security Council cease-fire resolution. Behind this action was a Kissinger-Brezhnev agreement to pressure both Israel and Egypt to stop the fighting. The detente at last seemed to be taking hold. Almost immediately, however, violations by Egypt and Israel led to the worst crisis since 1970. As a second UN cease-fire went into effect on October 24, word reached Washington of four more Soviet divisions placed on the alert, for a total of seven. Some 85 Soviet ships were counted in the Mediterranean, a dozen Antonov-22 transports were seen flying southward, and an airborne command post was known to have been set up in southern Russia. Moscow now proposed a joint US-Soviet peacekeeping force, but Washington rejected this gambit. During the evening of October 24, Brezhnev sent Nixon a coldly-worded letter that threatened the "taking of appropriate steps unilaterally. Israel cannot be allowed to get away with the violations . . . The United States and the USSR were on a collision course."[11] A top-level US meeting decided on a Defense Alert Condition Three. The alarm was reinforced by CIA reports that the USSR was landing nuclear weapons in Egypt. By midday of October 25, the USSR had begun to back off from its go-it-alone tactic. The 15-hour crisis was easing, and, as the Kalbs put it, "After a frightening exercise in nuclear muscle flexing, the two superpowers returned to the twilight zone of detente."[12]

Two conflicting assessments of the impact of US-Soviet detente upon the Middle East crisis are possible, and it is the nature of the detente that both have validity. The first views the detente as having bent under the strain of age-old and well-nigh intractable conflicts, but also as having held together and eventually provided a resolution

---

[10] *Christian Science Monitor*, March 12, 1974.
[11] Kalb and Kalb, *loc. cit.*
[12] *Ibid.*

of the crisis short of nuclear holocaust. Detente as a communication process permitted the two superpowers to confer and negotiate throughout the emergency; and when neither could risk going any further, United Nations machinery was brought into play effectively. In this view, the United States did not come off badly. The Egyptians, and to a lesser extent the Syrians, turned to the Americans as the only power that could talk to both the Arabs and the Israelis, thus pushing the USSR away from the center of decisionmaking and enhancing the role of the United States as a regional mediator. Without the previous growth of detente, there might have been no stopping the headlong rush to general war. This view is bolstered by the subsequent steady, if erratic, movement toward some composition of Arab-Israeli differences since October 1973.

The other assessment takes a different angle of vision. When push came to shove, detente could operate only *after* an old-fashioned military showdown. Brezhnev did not decide to back away from his unilateral threats because of the spirit of detente or the other benefits he expected to derive from it, but because of the American military alert and all its implications. While it is true that the US and Soviet leaders never stopped talking, it is also true that their countries were engaged in war by proxy. From October 13 to November 14, 1973, the USSR supplied between 200,000 and 225,000 tons of war material and other help by sea alone, in addition to what was sent by air. During the same period, the US Air Force flew over 22,000 tons of equipment to Israel.[13] Talk-*and*-fight, not talk-*or*-fight, was the order of the day. At a certain point, talk failed to contain the tensions, and the contest became one of arms, power, and will. When that confrontation was decided, talk could regain its primacy. But any satisfaction that the two superpowers did not, after all, go over the brink had to be tempered by two facts that emerged in retrospect: detente did not avert the potentially deadly clash in the first place; and when it came, the conciliatory processes of detente had to stand idly by while policy, in Clausewitz's phrase, was carried on by other means.

In theory, there is no reason why something from each assessment cannot be abstracted and synthesized. In practice, the validity of any

---

[13] *New York Times*, November 28, 1973.

such synthesis would depend on what came after the 1973 crisis. If both major powers had moved away from further collision, the two assessments could be taken as balancing each other out. The trouble is that while the United States has moved perceptibly away from Israel, urging it to make sizable concessions to the Arab states, while at the same time encouraging Egypt and Jordan to start indirect negotiations with Israel, there is no sign that the USSR has modified its strategic approach to the Middle East and its tensions. Tactically, Moscow helped secure the Syria-Israel disengagement in May 1974. At the same time, Brezhnev asserted in a message to President Assad of Syria that the accord "sets the beginning of liberation of Syrian territory occupied by the Israeli invaders . . . Disengagement of troops is no doubt but a first step along the road towards a final Middle East settlement, the core of which must be the withdrawal of Israeli troops from all Arab lands occupied in 1967 and safeguarding the legitimate national rights of the Arab peoples."[14]

Brezhnev's assurances are a prescription for further conflict and further strain on the detente. Egypt and Jordan cannot by themselves make a lasting peace with Israel; Syria, too, must be a party. A year after the 1973 war, however, Russia was encouraging Syria to hold out for total Israeli capitulation. Meanwhile, a $2 billion Soviet arms program had made the Syrian forces one of the most formidable, if not the strongest, in that part of the world. The Syrian build-up and the Israeli "practice" mobilization of August 1974 showed how fragile were the barriers to a new crisis.

Thus, Middle East crisis management as an application of Soviet-American detente raises questions about the fundamental nature of detente itself. In his 1973 year-end press conference, Kissinger took —for him—rare note of these questions. Speaking of the Middle East, and addressing the USSR as much as the questioner in the audience, he said: "It is not possible for a country to exacerbate tensions in one area and to seek relaxation in another. This Administration has consistently opposed the notion of selective detente." Looking back on the expectations of a year and a half earlier, he remarked that the benefits of detente "are taken for granted, and . . .

---

[14] USSR Mission to the United Nations, *Press Release No. 39*, May 31, 1974.

some of the difficulties that were overlooked in the beginning become more and more apparent."[15] The International Institute for Strategic Studies noted in its own review of 1973 that "the limits of detente" had been reached and exposed in the Middle East conflict.[16]

A second cluster of questions also arises, going much deeper than the events of 1973 in the Middle East. How does the Soviet leadership reconcile its evident desire for detente with its equally evident determination to foment further challenges to detente? Is this some cynical duplicity and deception, founded on a belief that Soviet policy can have it both ways? Or, is there some inner ideological recess where the two thrusts come together in what seems to the Soviet leadership as a perfectly logical and ethical blend? These questions will require a closer examination later. For now, it may be noted that different perceptions of detente, as well as different strategic interests, stood out sharply in the Middle East emergency. In the light of this, the next immediate question is, Where does the rest of the detente fit in, particularly the substantial flow of US trade, technology, and credits that was undertaken as an antidote to such perils as erupted in the Middle East?

---

[15] Department of State, *Secretary Kissinger's Year-End Review*, December 27, 1973.
[16] Quoted in *New York Times*, May 10, 1974.

# 4

## The Trade Bridge

In October 1973, as Soviet and American troops went on alert, and crisis management in the Middle East was on the verge of breaking down altogether, some 200 American firms "spent $12 million to show their wares at the nine-day Nafta-Gaz (gas and oil) exhibit in Moscow's Sokolniki Park."[1] If the US and USSR could not reach a mutually acceptable arms control pact, and if their detente was bending under the strain of the Middle East crisis, still they were succeeding with trade and aid. In fact, they were succeeding far better than a growing list of critics believed was tolerable.

There was little hint of what lay ahead when the Big Two wrote the "Commercial and Economic Relations" section of the 1972 agreements. "The two sides," the prosaic text read, "agree that realistic conditions exist for increasing economic ties. These ties should develop on the basis of mutual benefit and in accordance with generally accepted international practice." This last meant Soviet treatment as a "most-favored nation," that is, getting the same tariff breaks as America's other trading partners. MFN was tied to discussion of wartime Soviet Lend-Lease debts. A US-Soviet Joint Commercial Commission was to begin the practical work of arranging for the trade deals.[2]

No questions on this subject came up in Kissinger's meeting with the reporters, whose attention was mainly on the arms control pro-

---

[1] Harvey D. Shapiro, "Alexei Kosygin Has a Friend at Chase Manhattan." *New York Times Magazine*, February 2, 1974.
[2] *Presidential Documents*, p. 946.

visions. The economics of detente seemed unexceptionable. Trade and other forms of economic transfer had been part of every detente since 1920. Moreover, whatever strides the USSR had taken to match or exceed the US in military power, it was hopelessly lagging in economics. Here, then, was a concrete reason for the new optimism that Soviet-American relations were at last becoming normalized.

The first traffic over the new trade bridge shook the structure noticeably. In July 1972, the US sold the USSR $750 million of American grain. Commodity Credit Corporation officials smiled as midwestern bins were emptied of their surpluses. The Treasury Department hailed the reduction and disappearance of the country's adverse balance of payments in international trade. Detente had returned an early and welcome dividend. The gratification, however, was shortlived. As the price of wheat on the world market rose well above the $1.65 the Russians had paid per bushel, the deal began to look like a bad one for US farmers. For consumers, the impact was much more severe. Under the pressures of rising wheat prices and shrinking world supplies, bread prices rose far beyond the penny or two that officials had predicted. Not all the rise could be blamed on the grain sales, of course, but they were a visible cause. With bakers talking about dollar-a-loaf bread, the average citizen was getting a pointed lesson in one of the costs of detente.

Nonetheless, the momentum of trade seemed unstoppable, outstripping the most optimistic forecasts. The Joint Commercial Commission worked through the Summer; and by October 18, an omnibus trade agreement was ready for signature. It provided for tripling Soviet-American trade in the period 1972-74, from $500 million a year to $1.5 billion. That goal was reached a year ahead of schedule, when the $640 million figure for 1972 more than doubled. The total dropped off somewhat in 1974 because a bumper Soviet harvest made further large grain imports unnecessary. As President Nixon went to Moscow in June, a billion dollar volume was still expected.[3]

In the first trade surge, American firms signed contracts for $400 million worth of equipment and machinery for the Soviet Kama River

---

[3] *New York Times*, June 23, 1974.

truck-manufacturing plant. A Kama Purchasing Commission was set up in New York in 1973. A further $300 million for an ammonia and urea fertilizer factory in Kuibyshev was also being negotiated. Some 1,200 "co-production" agreements were initiated, under which the US and USSR would jointly establish and operate the facilities and the United States would get a share of the output. The best known was a plan for joint exploitation of natural gas deposits in Soviet Siberia. All of these projects were dwarfed by Occidental Petroleum's announcement of an $8 billion, 20-year project for manufacturing fertilizer in the USSR. (Occidental's head, Armand Hammer, had been one of Lenin's closest foreign collaborators in the early 1920s, serving as the middleman who brought Ford tractors and other enterprises to Russia.)

Extractive and heavy manufacturing industries were only the top of the Soviet shopping list. Control Data Corporation was approached for $500 million of sophisticated computer equipment and know-how. An entire US jet airplane plant was requested. As a *New York Times* correspondent remarked in reporting on this aspect of the trade surge, "Soviet hunger for advanced industrial techniques seems insatiable as the Kremlin makes up for years of neglect in research and development."[4] Food and other consumer products all seemed to find a ready market in the USSR. Soviet citizens would be drinking Pepsi Cola, and Americans would get Stolichnaya vodka in return, under a contract concluded by Pepsico's Chairman, Donald Kendall. American industrial designer Raymond Loewy is working on Russian automobiles, motorcycles, sports hydrofoils, and other advanced consumer favorites.[5]

Not the least striking development was the alacrity with which American businessman hurried to embrace Soviet industrial bureaucrats. Almost five months before the 1974 summit meetings, the first full meeting of the Board of Directors of the US-USSR Trade and Economic Council was held in Washington. The Board consists of the chief executive officers of 26 major corporations, and an equal number of Soviet trade officials. It has two Honorary Directors, the US Secretary of the Treasury and the Soviet Minister of Foreign Trade.

---

[4] *Ibid.*
[5] Shapiro, *loc. cit.*

Annual dues of between $1,000 and $10,000, scaled to the volume of company sales, are paid by the American firms and matched by an equal amount from the Soviet Government. Co-Chairmen are Donald M. Kendall, Pepsico head, and Vladimir S. Alkhimov, Deputy Foreign Trade Minister of the USSR.[6]

The Council describes itself as "the product of detente," an outgrowth of "government-to-government agreement (that) recognized the need for a specialized binational organization to help bridge the Cold War gap that had separated both countries for more than a quarter of a century." It offered all kinds of services in locating markets, arranging contracts, providing research and information, and logistical support. From the wording of its brochure, as well as the composition of its management, it is obvious that the Council also functions as a high-powered interest group, both organizationally and individually by members, to promote and expand trade between the two countries. Kendall, for example, has been most prominent in American public affairs forums supporting not only more trade but the general concept of detente itself. His efforts have been seconded by the others on the Council, notably Chamber of Commerce President Arch Booth and David Rockefeller, Chairman of the Chase Manhattan Bank.[7]

If economics and trade were the whole of detente, or even a determining part, the Nixon-Kissinger initiatives would be beyond cavil. But unfortunately, that is not the case, as the London *Economist* pointed out in one of its more critical commentaries, just before the 1974 summit:[8]

> Everyone lived happily, if not ever after, at least for a while. American exports to Russia increased from about £67m in 1971 to more than £490m in 1973. About 45 percent of this was financed by the Export-Import bank at six percent interest, well below commercial rates. And American imports from Russia rose to almost £90m, more than twice that of any previous year, but still a miniscule portion of American trade.

---

[6] US-USSR Trade and Economic Council, Inc., *The New Trade Opportunity*. Undated.
[7] *Ibid.*
[8] *Economist*, May 11, 1974.

But then last October's war in the Middle East set a lot more Americans wondering just what detente was all about, in addition to those who had been skeptical about it from the start. To many of them, it seemed to be nothing more than a lot of grain (which had been heavily subsidized in the first place) sold on terms that looked scandalously low in late 1973, and a bunch of IOUs in the Export-Import bank's till, given in return for valuable technology.

"Detente it isn't," the *Economist's* caption read.

These two paragraphs get to the essence of the trade issue: attractions and benefits versus costs and consequences. The reaction to the grain deal had given some warning that trade with Russia was not universally regarded as a boon, but this was only a portent. Debate and polarization did not really begin to take shape until the October 1972 accords brought the questions of most-favored-nation status and Export-Import Bank credits into full view. The October agreement made explicit the implied June promise of MFN standing for Russia. At the same time, President Nixon made an official determination that trade with Russia was in the US national interest, a move required to permit the Bank to extend the credits Russia needed to pay for its purchases.[9]

The storm that followed completely shattered old ideological lines. Traditional pro- and anti-accommodation groupings were forgotten as leaders in every walk of public life did battle around MFN and the Ex-Im Bank. Liberals and conservatives of all shadings were side-by-side against the trade terms. Some of America's foremost capitalist-imperialist captains found themselves allied with revisionist professors and *Pravda*, all arguing in favor of the proposed terms. Anyone absorbed in the debate over Vietnam who suddenly turned to the public discussion of the Trade Reform Bill in 1973 would have been thoroughly bewildered by the new line-ups.

Liberal Senator Case of New Jersey, a leading opponent of US involvement in Vietnam, led off the attack by demanding to know

---

[9] The Bank was established by President Roosevelt in 1934, also to provide trade credits to the USSR. Nothing came of that plan, but the Bank continued to extend credits to other countries, mainly for US exports.

why the Administration had failed to submit the October agreements to Congress. Another liberal Senator, Schweiker of Pennsylvania, challenged the legality of Nixon's declaration of "national interest," and asked the General Accounting Office to rule on it.[10] Equally liberal Senator Stevenson of Illinois questioned Ex-Im Chairman William J. Casey sharply in Senate hearings. What if the USSR refuses to pay back the loans? Won't the Kama trucks compete with American products in world markets? How do we know the USSR will honor its promises to give the US a share of the fertilizers due under the Occidental Petroleum deal? Will all this trade actually lead to the improvement of US-Soviet relations? Stevenson was particularly insistent on developing the difference between the six percent interest charge Russia was paying and the 7.3 percent rate prevailing in world money markets—a 1.3 percent "subsidy" paid for by US taxpayers.[11] Another opponent of Vietnam policy, Professor Hans Morgenthau, wrote in the *New Leader* that economic help to the USSR, without any assurance as to how it would be used, was to give the USSR a "breathing spell in an ongoing struggle for total stakes."[12]

In the House of Representatives, skeptics led by Representatives Vanik and Mills introduced an amendment to the Trade Reform Bill that would deny MFN status to the USSR unless it loosened restrictions on emigration from Russia. On December 11, 1973, this amendment passed by a vote of 319 to 80. Some of the supporters were motivated primarily by moral repugnance, but the amendment served as a rallying point for all varieties of opposition. In the Senate, Senator Jackson of Washington submitted his counterpart of the Vanik-Mills amendment, a companion to his earlier resolution which put Congress on record in calling for genuine equality in the next round of strategic arms negotiations.

Attacks on the trade bill held up passage and led to extensive hearings on the Jackson amendment in the Senate. On March 27, 1974, the Finance Committee heard a strong denunciation of detente trade policy from George Meany, President of the AFL-CIO:

---

[10] *Economist*, May 11, 1974.
[11] *New York Times*, April 7, 1974.
[12] Hans J. Morgenthau, "The Danger of Detente," *New Leader*, October 1, 1973, p. 6.

Too many American businessmen and bankers are shortsighted when they forget that commercial relations with the Soviet Union are not ordinary and normal trade deals between buyers and sellers in the free world. The Soviet government has a total monopoly on the buying and selling of all goods and access to all raw material resources in the USSR. American technological know-how turned over to Russia stays there and helps develop its resources. The Soviet rulers can shut off their markets or natural resources at any time they see fit. The benefits of US technological help to the Russians are permanent, and will sooner or later reduce Russia's need for buying from the US.

Meany was even more blunt in speaking to the International Machinists Union that evening. "Let's look at this thing they call detente— this fraud they call detente . . . Let me tell you, I don't know whether it is hot or cold, but we still have the war. And detente is merely a facade for that war. It is a phony; it is a real phony."[13] In a similar vein, Representative Ichord of Missouri told the House Banking Commitee: "If I were a businessman, I would probably sell my goods to my enemy if I could make a profit; but I'll be damned if I would loan him the money to put me out of business."[14]

The defenders of detente trade policy fought back with equal intensity. In March 1974, Secretary Kissinger testified before the Senate Finance Committee that linking Soviet trade benefits with issues like human rights would imperil detente, and might lead to a total stoppage of Jewish emigration from the USSR. He said his own Jewish background made him especially aware of the humanitarian considerations, but that the other reasons for seeking detente were overriding: the prevention of nuclear catastrophe, working toward world peace, and reducing armaments. Kissinger also argued that the half billion dollars thus far granted in Export-Import Bank credits were for the benefit of US businessmen, who had to have financial support if they were to enter Soviet markets. Furthermore, he pointed out, without MFN the USSR would not repay $722 million in Lend-Lease debts.[15]

---

[13] AFL-CIO Press Release, March 27, 1974.
[14] American Security Council, *Washington Report*, February 1974.
[15] *Christian Science Monitor*, March 8, 1974.

Ex-Im Bank Chairman Casey came before the same committee in April. He testified that the Soviet credits amounted to no more than 1.7 percent of the Bank's total loans, and that if all Soviet lending were cut off, the Bank would not feel it too much. He conceded that the credit decision was "political," that is, it was part of overall detente policy, but he also declared that "a lot of good business for the US" was involved. Another Ex-Im official estimated that "there is $120 billion worth of business out there in the next four years, and we want our share."[16]

Perhaps the most dramatic shift of posture was by the great corporate leaders. Chase Manhattan's David Rockefeller contended that an expansion of trade and commerce, far from increasing Soviet intransigence, would ameliorate international tensions and modify the domestic Communist system. Control Data's Chairman, William C. Norris, said that the Eastern bloc countries did not "desperately need" US exports, and could get what they needed from other countries. Restrictions by the United States would result only in depriving this country of both expanded profits and the one chance to influence Soviet behavior. The industrial leaders made the further argument that the Communists were good financial risks. Rockefeller declared that they were scrupulous in paying their bills on time. A Shell Oil executive was quoted as saying that Russia's gas-oil Nafta was "interested above all in profits." And Armand Hammer went further than all the others when he remarked: "Very seldom do businessmen have a chance to make history."[17]

The Soviet Union reacted to this debate in its own fashion, not without some noticeable contradictions. First, it carefully separated friend from foe in the United States. A *Pravda* article of January 29, 1974, accused Pentagon "economists" of working to prove that "American businessmen allegedly stand to lose from trade with the Soviet Union." But, it added, the businessmen were too sophisticated not to see the mutual profitability of US-USSR economic relations. The Soviet paper attacked the Pentagon's research director, Malcolm Currie, for seeking to hinder technological

---

[16] *New York Times*, April 7, 1974.
[17] Shapiro, *loc. cit.*

cooperation under the guise of the "national security" argument. *Pravda* hinted that the USSR might have to seek alternate sources of help.[18] This is an old Soviet technique; it is still used to praise President Roosevelt while denouncing those who sought to sabotage his plans for improving relations between the two nations. Moscow also applied it to President Nixon, whom it portrayed as the victim of the American news media. The argument conveniently overlooks the fact that the Pentagon and its personnel were also the instruments of the same President Nixon.

Second, the USSR kept its eye on the main objective, more resource transfer. In May 1974, eight members of the Supreme Soviet came to Washington and staged what *New York Daily News* columnist Jerry Greene described as "a remarkable demonstration of lobbying, American style, for the pending trade bill and for eternal peace and friendship." Wrote Greene: "The delegation was overflowing with charm and laughter, working at this detente business as if their jobs and even their lives depended upon it."[19]

On a third level, at least some of this eagerness started to cool. Deputy Chairman Gvishiani, of the Soviet State Committee for Science and Technology, told American newsmen on March 27, 1974, that the USSR had "no immense need" to sell its Siberian gas and oil to the United States, and would not do so unless the US was willing to put up the money—estimated at over $6 billion.[20] His warning was in part a recognition that the Siberian project had little chance of approval by the United States. The total of $6 billion to build facilities that would remain under Soviet control, and which would help turn Siberia into a power base for Russia's Far Eastern armies and fleet, was more than most prodetentists cared to pursue. Gvishiani's warning was also motivated by the changing economics of energy production, which saw Soviet output rise ten percent in 1973 while profits went up by 44 percent. Denmark, for example, bought 139,000 fewer tons of Soviet oil in 1973, but paid out more than three times what it had in 1972.[21] Russia had evidently taken a leaf from the Arab book.

---

[18] *New York Times,* January 30, 1974.
[19] *New York Daily News,* May 23, 1974.
[20] *New York Times,* March 27, 1974.
[21] *Ibid.,* June 5, 1974.

Finally, as a *Chicago Daily News* correspondent reported from Moscow in June 1974, some of the bloom was off the rose of business relations. Not only were the costs of living exorbitant—"Here for $50 a day you get a dump with no service"—but they were being applied discriminatingly against Americans. Office space was scarce, secretarial and other pay was more than three times the going Russian rate; and when the Americans complained, they were told to take it or leave it. "If you didn't want to pay, you shouldn't have come."[22]

By the end of 1974, the trade-detente controversy had come to an equilibrium of sorts. In October, Secretary of State Kissinger sent Senator Jackson a letter stating that the Soviet Union had agreed to ease restrictions on emigration. Jackson replied that the US would apply a "benchmark" of 60,000 visas a year for would-be emigrants, irrespective of their "race, religion, or national origin." The way was open now for Jackson and his colleagues to drop their opposition to MFN status for the USSR. At the same time, agreement was announced whereby the USSR would be permitted to buy 2.2 million metric tons of American grain before June 30, 1975,[23] much less than the 3 million tons or more that Moscow had been trying to buy.

Congress passed the Trade Reform Act, and the President signed it on January 3, 1975, but its contents were well short of what the Administration and the Soviet leaders had envisioned. Most-favored-nation treatment was to be extended to the USSR, but for 18 months, not three years, and contingent for renewal upon Soviet performance in permitting emigration. Export-Import Bank credits were also extended for one and a half years, but were limited to $300 million, not the $1 billion the Russians had expected. Kissinger tried to soften the impact these restrictions would inevitably have on the USSR, warning the Senate Finance Committee that continued public commentary on Jewish emigration and on who won or lost would imperil not only US-Soviet trade relations, but the entire detente.[24]

---

[22] *New York Post*, June 4, 1974.
[23] *New York Times*, October 20, 1974.
[24] State Department Bureau of Public Affairs, "Statement of Secretary of State Kissinger Before the Senate Finance Committee on the Trade Reform Act, December 3, 1974," p. 3.

Soviet unhappiness surfaced in mid-December when Tass, the USSR press agency, issued a statement calling the trade-emigration tie in the bill then still pending an attempt "to interfere in the internal affairs" of the Soviet Union. Boris Ponomarev, who heads Soviet relations with Communist Parties in the West, told a meeting in Budapest that trade "promotes the struggle" by helping workers hurt by the recession in the West, and called for sharpening of the ideological conflict.[25] Leonid Zamyatin, the Director-General of Tass, threatened that the USSR might review its entire trading relationship with the US and direct its business elsewhere. He blamed the obstacles on "opponents of detente" within the United States.[26]

Zamyatin's threat was carried out on January 10, 1975, when the Soviet government notified the United States that it would not put the 1972 trade agreement into effect. After four days of trying to get the USSR to reconsider its decision, Kissinger announced on January 14 that the US would halt its own steps to apply the agreement. Cancellation of the trade pact meant that the USSR would not receive MFN status or further export-import credits, nor would it repay almost $700 million in World War II Lend-Lease debts. As a practical matter, these losses were not significant; but symbolically, one of the main—and thus far more successful—underpinnings of the detente had dissolved in a further exposure of its limits.

On balance, however, the USSR had reason for satisfaction and for assuring President Ford that it wanted the detente to go on. As one group of 12 specialists on Soviet and international affairs pointed out in a statement reprinted by Senator Jackson's subcommittee, the inflow of American technology and financing would benefit the USSR substantially. The Control Data contract, for example, would cost $3 million over three years. For that, Moscow would gain 15 years in R&D computer technology. Yet, the US would have no access to anything the USSR was working on. As the group noted, American input would relieve much of the strain on the USSR as it tightened its internal controls further, sent its espionage agents abroad, and built up still further its already formidable military machine.[27]

---

[25] *New York Times*, December 22, 1974.
[26] *Ibid.*, December 29, 1974.
[27] US Senate Committee on the Armed Services, *Detente: An Evaluation* (1974).

The controversy over trade is unlikely to be settled to anyone's satisfaction. Much of it has been a dialogue of the deaf, with both sides talking past the other. The advocates of greater trade have relied basically on "what-could-be" arguments. Former Ambassador Harriman, for example, stated on June 18, 1974, that his talks with Brezhnev had convinced him that Brezhnev was sincere in seeking a reduction of tensions with the United States. The Jackson amendment had "outlived its usefulness" and should be dropped.[28] The opponents, on the other hand, stand on "what-is"—Soviet intransigence, ambition, and so on. Neither side has an altogether clear conception of what the relation of trade to detente ought to be. Kissinger and the responsible decisionmakers recognize that if trade and aid flourish while the rest of the detente remains bogged down or rolls backwards—which Harriman seems to accept—the net result could be new perils. On their part, the opponents are no more logical, since no trade should be approved with a nation perceived as an implacable foe.

Argument and rhetoric notwithstanding, detente has enforced a logic of its own in the trade sector. Success here, like the failures in arms control and crisis management, has exposed some of the true limits of detente. It has also brought to the surface once again what had been generally thought to be dead—the moral streak in American foreign policy. Trade has become not only a bridge between the United States and the Soviet Union, but also a bridge between the "practical" aspects of detente and the ethical imperative. Nobody planned it that way, but the humdrum details of dollars-and-cents economics became the catalyst that brought out a fundamental requirement of detente to this country: that it be more than just a relaxation between two superpowers armed for total destruction, and that it should also serve to alter the very character of the adversary. This is where the full burden of negotiation comes down—a point to be examined further.

---

[28] *New York Times*, June 18, 1974.

# 5

## Soviet Mellowing

Promoting democracy in other countries is not new to American foreign policy. Americans could never go west, subdue Southern rebels, cross the Pacific, or fight two world wars for reasons of naked power alone. It had to be for Manifest Destiny, the abolition of slavery, or the Four Freedoms as well. Whether this was hypocrisy or naivete, as the cynics here and abroad have called it, there is no mistaking the authentic responses that such imagery evoked among Americans.

The moral streak in present-day detente has some of this evangelism. Its fervor has dissipated over the years, and policymakers since John Foster Dulles have muted and suppressed it. But the residue still comes out as an aspiration that the US and USSR can share more common ideals, or at least some ground rules of behavior. To Americans, that seems sensible and innocent enough; to every Communist leader from Lenin on, such American aspirations have been seen as a threat, to be risked but carefully guarded against. To bring the USSR into closer contact with any alien system is to expose it to subversion, innocent or otherwise.

Residual evangelism is not the primary impetus behind the moral streak. Rather, it is the obverse: insecurity, fear, and defensiveness in the face of a USSR seemingly bent on overwhelming power and unwilling or unable to level off. There is the uneasy feeling that democracy's live-and-let-live approach to detente may be self-betraying when it confronts the singleminded activism of the Soviets. Mere detente may not be enough; something like a basic change in the Soviet system may be the *sine qua non* for any stable US-Soviet relationship. As detente runs into its natural limits, the impression left is that the Soviet Union has not changed, or at any rate has not changed enough to cease being a threat. This impression is reinforced by Soviet proclamations of unceasing ideological conflict, and eventually borders on American acceptance of the Leninist either-them-or-us hypothesis.

Thus, what George Kennan called the "mellowing" of the Soviet system has become an integral part of US detente policy. American officials rarely if ever put it in "should" terms, but as "would" or "will." Kennan, who has consistently opposed all forms of moralizing in foreign policy, forecast that when the USSR's expansionary thrust was "contained" by US power, it would inevitably evolve from within toward something more benign and, therefore, more easily lived with.[1] The proposition that democracies are inherently more pacific than dictatorships might not bear critical analysis; but it has become almost axiomatic in American thinking, and is not far in the background of the present detente.

Two questions arise from the moral streak in detente: Just what changes is the United States seeking to promote in the USSR? Are these changes getting closer, or are they receding? In analyzing both questions, it should be borne in mind that lines of thought are fuzzy and scattered on the first, while clear and generally accepted criteria for measuring the second are lacking. A number of conclusions may be drawn, however, from the voluminous discourse to date.

## US Objectives for Change

At first glance, the changes that the United States seems to want in the USSR are relatively mild and modest. Proponents fall into four general categories: those who seek broad and farreaching change; those who would like to see broad changes, but are reconciled to much narrower ones; those who would let changes come in their own way and at their own pace; and those who would discourage as

---

[1] (George Kennan), "The Sources of Soviet Conduct," *Foreign Affairs* (July 1947).

far as they could any goal of changing the Soviet system. Considering these in reverse order, following are some typical expressions in each category and what they imply.

*Very little change.* The greatest proponent in this category is the US government, which had literally to be dragooned into asking the USSR to ease restrictions on Jewish emigration. With very obvious reluctance, and making clear to the USSR that he was yielding only to irresistible Congressional pressures, Kissinger has given formal approval to emigration as a US policy goal. But as he also told the Senate Foreign Relations Committee, Congressional demands were "really jeopardizing our ability" to carry out further detente with the USSR, a point with which the Committee Chairman, Senator J. W. Fulbright, concurred. Kissinger said that the matter was one best handled by the President in his personal contacts with the Soviet leaders.[2] As mentioned earlier, Kissinger has also made no secret of his thorough aversion to linking emigration with trade.

Whatever concessions the Nixon Administration made to its critics on Soviet emigration, it held the line firmly on the next most agitating issue, the persecution of Russia's dissident intellectuals. When President Nixon was asked in his February 25, 1974, TV press conference how the expulsion of Alexander Solzhenitsyn would affect detente, he replied that he admired the Nobel Prize winner for his literary achievements and personal courage; and that if he "thought that breaking relations with the Soviet or turning off our policy of negotiation and turning back to confrontation would help him or help thousands of others like him in the Soviet Union, we might do that." Nixon then added that in the years of confrontation, men like Solzhenitsyn were sent to Siberia, not Paris. He concluded by asking, Do we want to go back to those times?[3]

Nixon's self-imposed restraint was even more bluntly stated by US Information Agency Director James Keogh in a controversy over Voice of America coverage of Solzhenitsyn's book, *Gulag Archipelago*. According to Washington columnists Rowland Evans and Robert

---

[2] *New York Post*, June 8, 1974.
[3] *New York Times*, February 26, 1974.

Novak, VOA had been ordered to play down the book, presenting some reviews and other commentary, but not the text. Despite urging by the US Embassy in Moscow to broadcast the text to the Russian people, as the British and Germans were doing, Keogh flatly refused. Senator Jackson denounced the Administration for caving in to the Russian leaders. Keogh replied to his critics in language almost identical with Nixon's: "The principal goal of American foreign policy is to effect the policies of other nations toward negotiations and away from confrontation, not to transform the domestic structure of those societies."[4] There is no indication thus far that President Ford's position is any different.

If the Nixon-Kissinger-Fulbright conception of detente had no obstacles, there is little doubt that the detente would be all business and no sentimentality. The three are what may fairly be called "detente-firsters." Anything that impedes the detente is to be resisted, short of an actual sellout. They are eminently practitioners of what they see as the art of the possible. They are ready to deal with the adversary on the basis of common interests. Changing his ways, or pressing for concessions that challenge his control over his own people, is not their goal.

*Change at its own pace.* Official Administration policy attains some of its clarity by skirting the collateral effects of detente, namely, the subversion of the Soviet system through increased contact and exposure. A large group of Soviet specialists, of whom Alexander Dallin is representative, not only recognizes these effects but embraces them. In an article in *Encounter*, Dallin, a former Director of Columbia University's Russian Institute, writes:[5]

> In the long run . . . the multiplication of contacts and exposure, over both bread and circuses, cannot but yield a slow, almost imperceptible cumulation of new attitudes, perspectives, and assumptions . . . it may promote among the next generation of "official" and "semiofficial" Russia a greater sense that it is to their advantage to get along with the outside world.

---

[4] Rowland Evans and Robert D. Novak, *New York Post*, March 7, 1974.
[5] *Encounter*, June 16, 1974.

Dallin's view is cautious but expectant. A similar set of expectations, but expressed in the negative, comes from Professor Brzezinski:[6]

> (We used to think of detente as bringing) an increasing sense of shared ideals, with many in the Communist countries looking to us for inspiration. Detente today, instead, is a conservative balance-of-power arrangement, devoid of any moral content.

Brzezinski goes beyond Dallin in the degree of change he thinks is possible in Russia. Both men, however, share two assumptions. First, neither is expecting a complete metamorphosis of the Soviet system and limit their view to a more harmonious meshing of Soviet and Western foreign policy conduct. Dallin sees it coming eventually. Brzezinski recommends a more active US role in bringing it about, by means of our bargaining power with trade.[7] Their second common assumption is that the meshing is attainable only through the processes of detente. In both respects, they are not at odds with US policy, but only with the narrowness of the limits under which it operates.

*Reluctant reconciliation.* A third group of specialists has much less faith in the induction potential of detente, but is also aware of its powerful appeal. They will not, or cannot, break with it. Hence, they accept it and its modest capacity for bringing about change in the Soviet Union. But they do not hide their conviction that half-way accomplishments are fraught with danger, and keep trying for greater ones.

Leopold Labedz, coeditor of the London *Survey*, a leading journal of Communist affairs, speaks for this group. In the *Social Democrat*, published by the League for Industrial Democracy, he makes this point:[8]

> If the West, in response to detente policy, provides unconditional means of escape for them each time the Soviet leaders find

---

[6] Quoted in *New York Times*, June 17, 1974.
[7] See his article, "The Economics of Detente: A U.S. Portfolio in the U.S.S.R.?" *New Leader*, August 5, 1974.
[8] Leopold Labedz, "Detente and Soviet Repression." *Social Democrat* (Fall 1973), pp. 27, 28.

themselves on the horns of a dilemma, there will be no incentive leading to an internal evolution in which these leaders would have to become more realistic by abandoning some of their Utopian totalitarian heritage, and by accepting both internally and externally a more civilized posture of real detente both *vis-à-vis* their own citizens and foreign countries.

The changes Labedz would like to promote include lowering the present high level of military spending, deepening the tension between the leaders and the Party *apparatchiki*, and weakening Brezhnev's internal and external power position. "It is in the sphere of culture and human rights that the real crux of future Soviet evolution lies." For all his emphasis on goals far greater than the other two groups have espoused, Labedz would also work toward them through detente, not outside it. "It would seem a good idea," he says, "for any economic concessions, such as the granting of the most-favored-nation clause, to be made dependent on periodic scrutiny of the Soviet performance and of whether the conditions attached to it are being observed." It is unlikely, however, that he anticipates very farreaching "conditions" to be attached, or changes to come about that are significantly greater than those foreseen by Dallin or Brzezinski.

In the same category—but with different techniques—is the stand taken by Freedom House, an organization that has been monitoring and promoting freedom since 1939 when, as the Committee to Defend America by Aiding the Allies, it led the movement to send American aid to Britain and France. Its 1973 Freedom Award was presented to a frequently-imprisoned Soviet dissenter on December 4, 1973, who accepted on behalf of 15 human rights activists in the USSR. The recipient, Professor Alexander Volpin, called in his speech of acceptance for much more active pressure on the USSR by the free world, and insistence that the USSR obey the rule of law in governing its own people.

Several guest speakers spoke in a similar vein. Freedom House's President, Harry D. Gideonse, made a short presentation address which emphasized the organization's determination to give public recognition and endorsement to the Soviet dissenters, despite the

"pragmatic" negotiations on detente, which he called "desirable."
Gideonse described the 15 Russians being honored in these terms:
"Yes, we call them dissenters, not dissidents. For 'dissident' somehow
implies the intention to disrupt or even overthrow a government.
The men and women we honor today seek nonviolent reform within
the system."[9]

Freedom House's carefully constructed position reveals some of
the agonizing that Americans go through in trying to serve all of their
aspirations. There was no question where the organization stood on
Soviet repression. At the same time, it—like most American insti-
tutional bodies—accepted the necessity for detente. The very act of
honoring Soviet rebels was recognized as a blow to detente. The
formula for walking the thin line in between was to endorse both
the detente (with reservations) and the 15 victims. It also specified
that they were "dissenters," not "dissidents," working for change, not
overthrow. Yet, Gideonse also left no doubt that Freedom House
was calling for the full set of changes—free speech, free assembly,
free dissent—at some unspecified time in the future, and in some
unnamed way that would not, apparently, wreck the detente.

*Transformation of the Soviet System.* All three positions thus far
sketched stop well short of projecting the disappearance of the Communist order in Russia. While the varying pressures they generate on
detente contain an ultimate threat to the Soviet status quo, the inhibi-·
tions are more notable than the initiatives. To find those who call
for the transformation of the Soviet system, one must turn to the
USSR itself and its band of intellectual revolutionaries. The West
promotes change in the USSR diffidently, almost surreptitiously,
driven to it by the realities of power politics. Meanwhile, Soviet
citizens are talking up and sacrificing for change out of pure conviction. The paradox is discomfiting to Western decisionmakers, who
rarely anticipate what detente will call forth, and never quite know
what to do about it.

Ordinarily, a figure like Alexander Solzhenitsyn would present no
insuperable problems. Exiles seeking to work sea-changes in their

---

[9] *Freedom At Issue* (January-February 1974).

homeland are not new to the West. They are sheltered, honored, and eventually reduced to controllable size. The trouble is that his plight has brought forcefully to Western attention the fact that there are thousands of others like him still in the USSR, and still working to change the ruling order in their country. What is more, they use the communication networks to goad the West constantly to join their cause; and they make no concessions to the detente, which they regard as an outright menace to that cause. There are deep differences among novelist Solzhenitsyn, historian Roy Medvedev, and physicist Andre Sakharov on what kinds of change are necessary. Solzhenitsyn would recapture Russia's Slavic past, Medvedev would purify Marxism-Leninism by breaking the Party's monopolistic rule; and Sakharov would develop Soviet-Western convergence in some version of Social Democracy.[10] But they all go far beyond what the United States government is prepared to adopt as policy. In addition to its other frailties, detente must bear the strain of denunciations by Soviet citizens on moral, ethical, political, and even practical grounds.

To take two or three of the most upsetting denunciations, Solzhenitsyn has scored American liberal Ramsey Clark and Britain's Labor Prime Minister Harold Wilson for following a double standard in ignoring Communist evils while criticizing the misdeeds of the West. This is not the language Western liberals, who are among the most ardent devotees of accommodation with the USSR, want to hear. Medvedev has a different set of changes in mind, equally impracticable to the West, although he is not as hostile to detente as the others. Medvedev has not broken with Leninist orthodoxy, which he believes should be rejuvenated in the USSR. It is hard to see much support in the West for such an objective, much as Medvedev himself is admired for his outspoken opposition. Sakharov is in some ways the most difficult of the Soviet opponents for Americans to deal with. In the foreword to a book of his statements, he writes:[11]

> I am not an opponent of detente, trade, or disarmament. To the contrary, in several writings I have called for just those things. It is precisely in convergence that I see the only way to the salvation of mankind.

---

[10] Rudolf L. Tokes, "The Dissidents' Detente Debate," *New Leader*, March 4, 1974.
[11] Quoted in *New York Times*, February 5, 1974.

But I consider it my duty to point out all the hidden dangers of a false detente or a capitulation detente, and to call for utilization of the entire arsenal of means, of all efforts to achieve real convergence, accompanied by democratization, demilitarization, and social progress.

In the Fall 1973, Sakharov publicly urged the US Congress to deny the USSR tariff and credit concessions until his country's leaders were ready to begin opening up their closed society. Coming from an active and articulate opponent within the USSR, that was an embarrassment. Nor was there much prospect that it would disappear, thanks paradoxically to the detente itself, which made the total silencing of such opposition less feasible to the Soviet rulers.

## Change in the USSR

Measuring change is difficult in open societies; in the Soviet Union, it borders on the impossible. Not only are the instruments of measurement crude, the criteria in dispute, and the data scarce or unreliable. Changes in the Soviet system are also generally hidden from view until they burst forth as surprises. Not all the experts, for example, foresaw the demise of Beria, and some did not appraise correctly the extent of Khrushchev's difficulties just before his downfall. The efforts to rationalize Soviet economic behavior have been poorly charted in the West, to say the least. Detente may be having a far greater—or lesser—impact on the system than anyone suspects, or is able to discern. All that the outside observer can do is to work with the facts that are available, along the guideline suggested by Dallin: "It is naive to expect any early, dramatic, or profound changes in Soviet outlook, let alone their explicit acknowledgment from above."[12]

Some changes have inevitably taken place as a result of, or stimulated by, the detente, and others may be germinating. President Nixon was correct in saying that dissenters are being treated much more leniently now, and this is a change that the Soviet leadership did not

---

[12] Alexander Dallin, "All Orwellian Pigs?" *Encounter*, June 16, 1974.

make willingly. On January 7, 1974, Andrei Sakharov and four other Soviet intellectuals appealed to "decent people throughout the world" to protest the persecution of Solzhenitsyn.[13] Three days later, a Soviet television commentator for *Pravda* said that Solzhenitsyn and Sakharov were trying to play "martyr," but that it would not work.[14] Shortly thereafter, Solzhenitsyn was shipped out of Russia. Sakharov has not been punished to date for what has historically been regarded as treason in the USSR. Brezhnev himself dismissed him in March as "not a problem."[15]

Moscow's concessions on emigration should not be dismissed as negligible, either, whatever the number it allows to leave. It has backed off, tacitly at least, from its long-held insistence that emigration is "an internal matter." For a closed society inordinately suspicious of any outside attempt to intervene in its controls system, that is an unusual step. Moreover, the USSR is seen as yielding to pressure in the negotiating process—and from its *bete noire*, Henry Jackson, to boot. Despite Brezhnev's complaint about attaching "utterly irrelevant and unacceptable" conditions to trade agreements,[16] that is precisely what he attempted.

Russia's relatively circumspect attitude on the Cyprus crisis may also owe something to detente. The spectacle of two NATO members going to war with each other may have been reward enough, yet it is probably also true that the USSR did not want another showdown with the United States, particularly at a time when Washington was changing Presidents and Moscow was eager to tie the new incumbent down to continued trade and other benefits.

It is too early to assess the full dividends that may accrue. Some things will have to change as American high technology enters the Soviet mainstream in substantial volume. The computer might conceivably threaten Soviet dogmatisms more than the intellectuals ever could. Marxist-Leninist industrial bureaucrats have always had difficulty with Western-type managerial economics, and the influx now coming at them could compound their difficulties painfully.

---

[13] *New York Post*, January 7, 1974.
[14] *Ibid.*, January 10, 1974.
[15] *New York Times*, March 11, 1974.
[16] *Ibid.*, October 20, 1974.

Such gains and others that might flow from the detente are welcome to the United States. Against them must be counted all of the changes that have not taken place in the USSR, show no sign of taking place, and in fact now seem more unlikely than ever.

*Military thought.* If the Soviet civilian leaders couple their displays of weapons with calls for disarmament, their military colleagues are almost totally unyielding. Soviet field and flag officers write a great deal in the high-policy area; and while such men are expected to be "hard-liners," the extent of their aggressiveness is in striking contrast to the phrases of detente coming from the civilians.

War, and particularly nuclear war, is nowhere "unthinkable." Stability and stalemate are not part of the lexicon of Russia's military intellectuals, as they are of America's. Mutual Assured Destruction has no place; only destruction of the enemy is discussable. Wars will not be unleashed by the USSR, but by the imperialists, writes Colonel Yevgeny Rybkin in *Communist of the Armed Forces*, so that "it would be premature to announce the limitation of the possibility of the use of nuclear weapons in case the aggressor unleashed a war."[17] Colonel T. Kondratkov declares that "a third world war with the employment of nuclear weapons . . . would be (for the Socialists and other progressive states) a forced, legitimate, and just opposition to the criminal action of world reaction."[18] Nor, warns Colonel Krasnov, will the USSR wait for the "aggressor" to launch his weapons. What he calls the "surprise factor"—translatable as "first strike"—is an integral part of Soviet doctrine intended to assure victory.[19]

Not only are more devastating wars high on the Soviet "thinkable" list, the category of "just wars"—those the USSR will support—has grown larger and changed character subtly. Colonel Rybkin, in the article previously referred to, reaffirms old Soviet definitions of "just wars" as those in defense of the Soviet homeland, "national liberation wars" in developing countries, and two varieties of civil wars. He then adds: "Under certain conditions, defensive wars of the

---

[17] US Air Force, *Soviet Press Selected Translations*, no. 74-1, January 31, 1974, p. 8.
[18] *Ibid.*, no. 74-3, March 29, 1974, p. 20.
[19] *Ibid.*, no. 74-4, April 30, 1974, p. 42.

bourgeois nations can be just, if those nations are invaded by a stronger imperialist aggressor."[20] Under this broadened license, it is hard to envision any war anywhere in the world in which the USSR would now inhibit itself from intervening on the ground that it was not a "just war," either before or after the onset of hostilities. By extending the rationale for intervention from helping "Socialist" victims of capitalist aggression to helping some capitalist nations against others, the USSR has staked its claim to a global hand, and possibly more.

These are not simply verbal exercises by soldiers. They reflect Defense Minister Marshal Grechko's oft-quoted assertion that "the balance of world forces has changed in favor of the Soviet Union." Grechko, unlike his American counterparts in the military, is a sitting member of the Politburo, a policymaker and a spokesman for one of the main engines of political power in the USSR. There is little doubt about his and his subordinates' views of detente.

Soviet militarism at the highest political levels alone would be a formidable barrier to genuine detente. But that is only one part of a cast of thought that pervades the entire ruling structure all the way down to the education of children. The military training of Soviet youth is an old practice that began in Lenin's day. After World War II, as Leon Goure points out, it more or less lapsed as a compulsory affair and was taken over by a voluntary society known as DOSAAF, which worked with the *Komsomol* (Youth) organization, the Defense Ministry, the trade union councils, civil defense, sports, and other institutions at every level. In the 1960s, pressure to expand military indoctrination was stepped up sharply. At the present time, Goure reports, "some 71.5 million young people in the five-to-nineteen age group (are) involved, including 8.8 million boys sixteen to nineteen years of age, that is, in the group subject to compulsory preconscription military training."[21] The training includes not only the regular routine of military exercises but all of the thought-conditioning that goes with it, and concentrating especially on the threat from the imperialist powers led by the United States.

---

[20] *Ibid.*, no. 74-3, March 29, 1974, p. 20.
[21] Leon Goure, *The Military Indoctrination of Soviet Youth* (New York: National Strategy Information Center, 1973), pp. 15, 20.

How deeply such conditioning takes hold is open to question, as Goure remarks. Soviet youth, like most other young people, does not ingest everything they are told. From the point of view of detente, however, the relentless propaganda from every agency of society about the rottenness of bourgeois values and the necessity of preparing to sacrifice life in a new holocaust is hardly compatible with a softening of relations with Russia's detente partners.

*Dissenters.* Sending Solzhenitsyn to Paris and leaving Sakharov and Medvedev physically untouched has tended to obscure the much less fortunate situation of many other Soviet protesters. In January 1974, General Pyotr Grigorenko's term in a mental hospital was extended for six months, despite private Soviet promises to release him. Grigorenko had been seized for his activities on behalf of Russia's Crimean Tatars, who are demanding that they be allowed to return to the homes from which Stalin expelled them during World War II. Novelists Vladimir Maksimov and Aleksandr Galich cannot get permission to visit their families abroad. Professor Volpin, in accepting the Freedom House award, listed a number of other victims whose plight should not be forgotten—among them Sinyavsky, Daniel, Pavel Litvinov, Valentin Horoz, and others.

In February 1974, the *New York Times*' chief foreign correspondent, C. L. Sulzberger, reported "a slow decline in the extent and degree of what was clearly a larger body of opposition in the USSR only a few years ago." The decline is the result of what Sulzberger calls "internal detente," which breaks up the resistance groups by jailing some, exiling others, permitting a few to emigrate, and so on. "Internal detente," says Sulzberger, can be a "mortal danger to the idea of dissidence as expressing individual freedom" if external detente is not "carefully regulated along the lines called for by Sakharov."[22]

As the time approached for President Nixon's visit to Moscow for "Summit Three" in June 1974, Soviet citizens attempting to enter the American Embassy were subjected to increased harrassment, despite repeated protests from Ambassador Walter Stoessel. Marriages with

---

[22] *New York Times*, February 13, 1974.

American citizens were frustrated or delayed, exit visas held up or denied, and Jews subjected to new persecutions. Requests from the Embassy to the State Department to take top-level action with the Soviet Embassy in Washington apparently got nowhere.[23] The detente was not to be jeopardized on the eve of the next summit.

*Soviet espionage abroad.* Police crackdowns on Soviet citizens do not brighten the detente for Americans, but they can at least be presented as defensive, even fearful, a sign that the detente may be having some effect on the closed Soviet society. When the same police, the KGB, reaches abroad to promote subversion and worse, detente is no longer merely helping the leaders to perpetuate their domestic rule, but also aids them in their multisided offensive against other countries, including their detente partners.

In a new book that updates the Soviet espionage story, author John Barron cites statistics of the (British) Institute for the Study of Conflict that reveal an increase of Soviet agents in Western Europe from 1,485 in 1963 to over 2,100 in 1973. Three out of four Soviet diplomats in NATO countries are part of the KGB network.[24] Most of the work of these agents never comes to light, of course; but when something does break, it is generally shocking to detente advocates. Early in 1974, for example, a KGB spy was exposed as a trusted confidante of West German Chancellor Willy Brandt, whose *Ostpolitik* paved the way for the Nixon-Brezhnev summits. The spy's reports went to General Yuri Andropov, head of the KGB, and aided immeasureably in preparing the Soviet leaders to deal with both Brandt and Nixon. Disillusionment with Brandt's policies was reinforced, and helped to bring about Brandt's resignation as Chancellor.[25]

Robert Conquest provides further insights into Soviet espionage and subversion abroad. In 1971, some 105 members of the Soviet Embassy in London were expelled after their plans for sabotaging military and water installations were uncovered. Soviet arms went to the Irish Republican Army for use in the Ulster disorders. In 1968,

---

[23] Evans and Novak, *New York Post*, June 10, 1974.
[24] John Barron, *The Secret Work of Soviet Secret Agents* (Pleasantville, N.Y.: Readers Digest Press, 1974).
[25] *Economist*, May 22, 1974.

Mexican officials found scores of thousands of dollars in the luggage of Communist Party officials returning from Moscow. Four years later, Brazilian inspectors made a similar find. Conquest writes that the Soviet hand was evident in coups against the established regimes in Egypt (1971), the Sudan (1971), Mexico (1971), Rumania (1972), Bolivia and Colombia (1972), and Yugoslavia (1974). All in all, some 380 Soviet "diplomats" have been expelled from 40 countries on all six continents since 1960—often to turn up soon after in neighboring capitals.[26]

It may be, as Barron suggests, that the KGB is working at cross-purposes with the Brezhnev leadership, trying to impede the detente out of opposition to an accommodation with the West. But as Conquest points out, the KGB is an integral part of the Soviet ruling apparatus, which has consistently honored its managers for their work. If Brezhnev cannot or will not reduce or eliminate its influence, any conflicts within the high command over its views are cold comfort to the United States. For whatever reason, the growth of espionage and sabotage activities abroad at the very time that detente is under negotiation is a matter of grave concern. Here, detente is producing neither mitigation nor change, and is quite possibly stimulating backward movement.

The state of change in the USSR led the *Economist* to make a cogent audit of detente in June 1974. "The whole question of detente with Russia has become inseparable from the sort of place Mr. Brezhnev's Russia is." Its judgment was that "late-Brezhnev Russia is a better place than Stalin's Russia was, but a worse one in most respects than the Russia of Khrushchev's last years." People live somewhat better now, but individual freedom is notably less. Economic reform, once looked to as an advance agent of change, has been discarded. Increased trade will only solidify resistance to change. The *Economist* suggests that some of the features of detente—arms control, crisis management—are worth pursuing, provided they are negotiated skillfully. Beyond that, it is "by no means evident that it

---

[26] Robert Conquest, "The K.G.B. Plays Dirty Tricks, Too." *New York Times*, September 29, 1974.

serves any Western interest to continue down the path of detente as Mr. Brezhnev defines it."[27]

If only the United States were involved, the risks of staying on that path might be more easily borne. But there are other effects of detente, on the Western alliance and on socalled Third World countries. They, too, must be put into the equation of aims and effectiveness.

[27] *Economist,* June 4, 1974.

# 6

## The Fallout on the Allies

### Western Europe

America's European allies did not need the Nixon-Brezhnev detente to turn them against the United States or one another. Frictions over sharing costs, troop-civilian hostility in French and German towns, and strategic policies have been endemic almost from the beginning. European fears of a US-Soviet "deal" to run Europe as a dual hegemony were well exploited by Charles de Gaulle after he became President in 1958. President Kennedy's espousal of a "flexible response" in the event of war was portrayed by de Gaulle and his spokesmen as a policy of "you fight, we talk." Would the US really risk Chicago to save Hamburg? Nor was the detente responsible for the panicky, every-man-for-himself reaction to the Arab oil embargo in 1973, or for tensions within the European Common Market.

Before taking up the effects that detente did have on the West European allies, it should be noted that the Europeans are ambivalent about the detente concept itself. Repelled as they are by the thought of being bypassed or endangered by it, they are also attracted by the promise of reduced arms burdens and new markets that detente seems to carry. Detente, therefore, has inevitably had both positive and negative effects on North Atlantic community morale and cohesiveness. But the negative have clearly outnumbered and outweighed the positive.

A staff report prepared for the Senate Foreign Relations Committee in September 1973 sums up the dissatisfactions in Europe *before* the blows from the 1973 Middle East War. Field investigators returned from Europe on October 4 saying, "Despite the apparent public desire in Europe to believe in detente, European leaders are highly dubious that long-term Soviet intentions have changed or that the Soviets are entering the MBFR negotiations in good faith."[1] Because of these fears, the report says, MBFR is not only a negotiation between the US and USSR, but also between the US and its NATO allies. "Can a proposal be developed," it asks, "which will be at once acceptable to our NATO allies and negotiable with the Soviet Union, or will any proposal which the Soviets might find acceptable be unacceptable to NATO?"[2]

There was a widespread belief among European leaders that MBFR was in any case no longer decisive, and that some US troops would be withdrawn from Europe in the next few years. Either negotiated or unilateral withdrawals would be equally disturbing to Europeans, because the troops are regarded as a tangible commitment to Europe's defense. "In recent months, this concern has been aggravated by the growing belief among Europeans that the United States is prepared to deal over their heads on security matters with the Soviet Union."[3]

Fears of US troop cuts are compounded by a corresponding drop in European public will. "As memories of World War II fade and talk of detente continues, virtually all NATO governments will be faced with a growing popular demand to share in force reductions and to cut defense budgets." West Germany is apprehensive that US cuts may not be matched by appropriate Soviet cuts. Britain is strongly opposed to MBFR, having recently "come into" Europe again. France, of course, views the American MBFR initiatives as yet another sign of lessened American concern for European defense.[4]

In the midst of these doubts and resentments, the Middle East War struck in October, followed by the Arab supply and price squeeze

---

[1] US Senate, Subcommittee on US Security Agreements and Commitments Abroad of the Committee on Foreign Relations, *Issues in Europe*, December 12, 1973, p. 26.
[2] *Ibid.*, p. 10.
[3] *Ibid.*, p. 13.
[4] *Ibid.*, pp. 11, 12.

on oil. "The Idea of Europe Runs Out of Gas," a Walter Laqueur
headline read. As Europe's leaders floundered in confusion and
Libya's Colonel Qaddafi spoke of converting this "geographical extension of Africa and the Middle East" to Islam, European bitter-
ness erupted against the United States. At the December NATO
meeting in Brussels, the US was scolded for humiliating Europe in
the Middle Eastern crisis by ignoring it. Secretary of Defense Schlesinger led a string of experts who told of growing Soviet military
power in Europe. But the NATO representatives said that they not
only could not get public support for more defense, but would
probably have to make cuts because of the higher cost of energy.
Right after Brussels, French President Pompidou called West European leaders to a summit meeting in Copenhagen as a protest against
US treatment of its allies. Four Arab foreign ministers also came,
uninvited, but were given royal treatment. Pompidou called for a
politically unified Europe, and predicted it would be realized by
1980.[5] It was unlikely that the European allies—including France—
would sever their ties with the United States. But their sharp criticism showed how far the Middle Eastern application of detente had
depressed NATO's inner unity and spirit.

Thus, on most of the main elements in detente—SALT, MBFR,
crisis management—the European allies felt excluded and irrelevant.
But there was one other element in which they had an indispensable
part and so could make their feelings effective—the Conference on
Security and Cooperation in Europe. The West Europeans had never
been enthusiastic about the 35-nation conclave that Brezhnev had
been promoting since the 1972 agreements put it on the agenda of
detente. Preparations lagged throughout 1972, and the Conference
was not formally launched until July 1973. As apprehensions over
US-Soviet dealings grew, West European insistence on genuine Soviet
concessions on human rights became more adamant. By the middle
of 1974, the West European stand on CSCE had become a virtual
backlash to the whole US-USSR detente.

Two ironies stand out in this picture. The first is that while many
in the United States, and very likely in the USSR as well, saw detente

---

[5] Walter Laqueur, "The Idea of Europe Runs Out of Gas." *New York Times Magazine*, January 20, 1974.

as ineffective and failing, the West Europeans saw it as succeeding much too well. The Security Conference seemed to them to cap insult with injury. Brezhnev would not only have his gains in strategic arms, his stronger hand in the Middle East, and his cozy relationship with his American friends, but there was also to be a great picnic to crown his efforts. America could bring its troops home. Russia's supremacy in Eastern Europe would be not only a fact of life, but also blessed by international sanction. Moreover, while the Red Army might not actually invade the West, Europe would in five years be, as one French official expressed it, "Finlandized." It could do whatever it liked in foreign and domestic affairs—so long as the USSR did not veto it. "We have a sense of another Munich," the official said.[6]

The second irony is that Nixon himself, whom West Europeans had generally regarded as a distasteful and compulsive anti-Communist, was not anti-Communist enough. The reason was not any change of heart, but Nixon's "need for another diplomatic coup," as the *Economist* phrased it, referring obliquely to Nixon's mounting impeachment troubles. "As the darkness deepens around Mr. Nixon, he appears to be fixing his eyes on the chink of light he sees in his projected journey to Moscow . . . (and) some diplomatic feat that could be cited to persuade people not to topple a President who is working hard, and successfully, for peace."[7] The Nixon-Brezhnev detente, in European eyes, had piled unworthy motives on top of unsound policy.

As the June 1974 summit approached, the Russians put on a brave face to hide their disappointment. In the last week of May, Kosygin announced that the Security Conference had achieved "definite results," and called for a grand finale to wrap it up. On the same day, the Dutch Foreign Minister, Max van der Stoel, spoke for the majority view that Russian intransigence on human and civil rights meant that "what was started in Helsinki so hopefully will end in disappointment in Geneva."[8] American spokesmen continued to say cautiously, right up to "Summit Three" itself, that the CSCE finale

---

[6] *New York Times*, December 2, 1973.
[7] *Economist*, June 1, 1974.
[8] *Ibid.*

was not yet to be ruled out; but they were wrong. The West European allies had made their point and were not about to retreat from it.

Western Europe's backlash to detente took place at the only point where it had any effective entry. Pique, retaliation, nationalistic pride all played their part in the tangle of motives. But the Europeans had also been guided by the same logic that had generated demands for change in the Soviet Union among US critics and Soviet dissenters. Unless the Kremlin leaders apply detente to their own subjects, given the military and economic gains they are scoring, the West will have little to show that the risks being taken were justified. As that logic had divided the Nixon Administration and its critics, so did it drive a new wedge into the European-American relationship, which already had plenty of other reasons for widening.

NATO did not break up over American detente conduct in the Middle East, nor will it. Both sides of the Atlantic need each other too much for that. As a third irony, the European partners discovered a new sense of solidarity, not against the adversary to the East, but in face of the partner to the West. To put it mildly, the net impact of detente upon the alliance was anything but salubrious.

**Vietnam**

Detente and disengagement from Vietnam were inextricably bound up with each other from the start of the first Nixon Administration. Nixon and Kissinger frequently reiterated the "linkage" between the two, making it clear that they expected the USSR to exert pressure on Hanoi to agree to a "peace with honor." Since much of the arms and material the North Vietnamese were using came from the Soviet Union, the necessary leverage was available. Moscow, the US assumption went, would place the accretion of detente benefits above all-out support for Hanoi, and cooperate with Nixon in what was his most obvious immediate need. In concrete terms, that meant a cease-fire without the prior departure of the Thieu regime in South Vietnam.

That was what Nixon and Kissinger hoped for and counted on. What they got was something less. Too little is yet known about the hidden discussions between the American and Soviet leaders, and what has begun to come out is embroiled in controversy. Certain things do seem evident, however. To begin with, the Russians were not overly impressed with "linkage," perhaps reasoning that the Americans needed them as much or more than they needed the Americans. They told Kissinger and Nixon repeatedly that they did not have the necessary influence over the North Vietnamese. By 1970, according to Bernard and Marvin Kalb, Kissinger was offering to drop the US demand that North Vietnamese troops be withdrawn from the South as a condition for a cease-fire. The Russians transmitted the offer, but the North Vietnamese continued to insist on the prior removal of Thieu.[9] A month before the May 1972 summit, Tad Szulc reported in a *Foreign Policy* article two years later, Kissinger went to Moscow secretly and renewed the offer, adding that all American civilians supporting the South Vietnamese forces would be withdrawn, and funds would be given to Hanoi for reconstruction. Again the Russians passed on the offer, but again disclaimed any power to make Hanoi accept it. The disclaimer was reemphasized by Brezhnev when he met Nixon in Moscow in May.[10]

What should have been for the Americans one of the shining accomplishments of the May agreements turned out instead to be an embarrassment. The Vietnam section of the protocols contained two separate and conflicting statements, in which the USSR carefully dissociated itself from any common stand. A second fact is self-evident; the cease-fire of January 1973 made no reference to North Vietnamese troop withdrawal. Kissinger has always insisted that no "secret agreements" were made, a claim that may be technically and legally correct, but which evidently left ample room for statements of "intent" that proved equally effective.

It seems safe to say that the Russians did act as mediators, or at least intermediaries, and probably urged Hanoi to accept Kissinger's offer and work for a more gradual erosion of Thieu's regime once the Americans were gone. (The Chinese were also enlisted and apparently gave the same advice.) In any event, Nixon and Kissinger were able to get a bare, livable minimum out of the Vietnam part of

---

[9] Marvin Kalb and Bernard Kalb, *Kissinger* (New York: Little, Brown, 1974), p. 134.
[10] Oswald Johnson in the *Washington Star-News*, June 2, 1974.

the detente, but at the price of storing up further trouble for themselves.

Theoretically, the North-South cease-fire has held up, but the fighting and the casualties have been severe. No Tet-type general offensive had developed by late 1974, but North Vietnamese military pressure on Saigon and Danang was intense and growing. North Vietnamese civilians also continued to move into the South, some 6,000 of them by March 1974, thereby establishing a permanent presence below the DMZ.[11] At the same time, the USSR strongly endorsed Hanoi's demands that American aid to the South be halted. Tass even claimed that the imperialists had reneged on their pledges to recognize two Vietnams in the South.[12] In the United States, too, Kissinger and Nixon were sharply criticized for keeping American civilians in Vietnam, a complaint that helped stimulate Congress to cut US aid to the Thieu government despite Ford Administration requests to maintain previous levels of support.[13]

In retrospect, it is possible to argue that detente gave North Vietnam as much as it gave South Vietnam or the United States, and quite possibly more. Soviet intermediation secured the Hanoi foothold, Soviet arms helped to extend it, and Soviet diplomatic support helped stave off compensatory US assistance to the South. The final chapter is not yet written.

### Germany

Willy Brandt's *Ostpolilik* has been in some respects an adjunct to the Nixon-Brezhnev detente, and in others its cutting edge. Three years before Nixon became President, Brandt, as Foreign Minister of West Germany, was moving toward his own detente with East Germany and its Communist bloc friends and sponsors. When he became Chancellor in the same year that Nixon was inaugurated as President, the two detentes began to mesh. Brandt's efforts to reduce cold war tensions between West Germany and Poland, Russia, and East Ger-

---

[11] *New York Times*, March 31, 1974.
[12] *Ibid.*, April 1, 1974.
[13] *Ibid.*, August 25, 1974.

many received cautious but clear approval in the West. The treaties he negotiated with Poland and the USSR, and pushed through to ratification in 1972, were welcomed as a vital part of the overall East-West thaw. There could be no lasting amity in Europe as long as West Germans harbored claims on lands occupied by Poland, or while West German-Soviet hatreds from World War II lay unburied.

Gratifying as Brandt's overtures were to a considerable body of opinion in the West, their key challenge came not from Russia or Poland, but East Germany. For the West Germans, if reunification was not in the cards, then visiting, travel, and other yearned-for contacts now seemed to be. For the Western powers, easing the divisions between the two Germanies promised the eventual diminution of Europe's most dangerous problem, Berlin. Distasteful as it was to Brandt and his Western allies to accept the legitimacy of the egregious "German Democratic Republic"—which Adenauer had always scornfully called the "Soviet Zone"—the price seemed worth paying for the returns promised.

A quarter of a century of crisis, confrontation, and all of the more subtle forms of Communist pressure had burned the naivete out of the Western negotiators. When the two detentes came together in the Four-Power Agreement of September 3, 1971, safeguards as well as concessions were written into the text. West Germany and its three allies conceded that West Berlin should not be an integral part of the Federal Republic and, as Bonn had maintained, governed from the West German capital. This was an important concession, since it went part of the way to meeting East Germany's undisguised intention of one day taking over all of Berlin. In return, the Agreement specified that "ties between the Western sectors of Berlin and the Federal Republic of Germany are to be maintained and developed." Additionally, overall responsibility for Berlin remained in the hands of the four occupying powers. An East German-West German transit agreement was also concluded, purportedly to end the harassments and stoppages on the land routes into Berlin. For his efforts, Brandt won the Nobel Peace Prize in 1971.

Like most of the other features of the broad detente, the 1971 pacts were less than fulfilled. They were never as popular in West

Germany as they appeared to be abroad—the Polish and Soviet treaties passed by two votes in the Bundestag. As the opening between the two Germanies proved to be so narrow that only a trickle of people could get through from East to West, disenchantment grew. Brandt sent his chief negotiator, Egon Bahr, to Moscow in March 1974 to take up the legal issues. Bahr was coldly received, and returned home with the issues unresolved.[14] In May, the spy scandal, coming on top of Brandt's other domestic woes, led to his resignation. The failure of detente to pay off for West German families still separated from relatives in the East was not the only cause of Brandt's downfall, but it was a strong contributory factor.

Brandt's departure left his successor, Helmut Schmidt, with a new crisis on the way. Bonn had, with allied approval, announced the establishment of an office of the federal environmental agency in West Berlin. Its purpose wás not so much to pursue clean air and water in Berlin as to make a stand on the 1971 "ties" before the East Germans hacked them to pieces with transit interference, harassments, and stoppages. Nothing like the 1948 blockade-airlift seemed in the offing—just the same petty squabbling that had masked the struggle for Berlin ever since the Allies had arrived there a generation earlier. In an editorial whose gloomy tone was typical of the let-down on detente throughout the West, one West German newspaper summed up the latest crisis as follows:[15]

> The pace of detente has slowed down considerably . . . and the latest Berlin dispute may well slow matters down still further. It is certainly difficult to reconcile with the hope of an imminent conclusion to the European Security Conference voiced in both East and West.

> Three years ago, the Four-Power Agreement was hailed as a major breakthrough in the search for a new relationship between East and West . . . Should the initial agreement on Berlin prove to have contained the seeds of further unrest, subsequent treaties will no longer look any too glamorous, either.

---

[14] *Ibid.*, March 10, 1974.
[15] *Koelner Stadt-Anzeiger*, July 23, 1974.

In distinct contrast, Politburo Member and chief ideological officer Mikhail Suslov pronounced himself satisfied with the state of detente. Speaking in Leningrad on the eve of the 1974 summit meeting, Suslov asserted that "the alignment of forces in the world has changed still further in favor of socialism, in favor of all the revolutionary-liberation and anti-imperialist forces." Peaceful coexistence has not merely brought about an easing of tension, it has done so on "Socialist" terms and to the advantage of socialism over its adversaries. Imperialist enemies still abound and the Socialist nations must remain strong and vigilant. But the "prestige of the Soviet Union in the international arena is now high as never before, and its foreign policy enjoys the trust of all honest people in the world."[16]

It goes without saying that a speech by a top Soviet leader is hardly an objective analysis of any situation. Suslov, moreover, is generally known as one of the Politburo's more skeptical members on detente, and his references to imperialist enemies are a pointed reminder to Brezhnev that detente still has a lot to prove. Nonetheless, the self-confidence Suslov expressed must be taken seriously, for two reasons. First, it would seem to find some corroboration in the pessimism so evident among Russia's Western adversaries. Second, and more important, to the extent that confidence is independent of fact, it points to a deeper source of leadership motivation and will. Like all viable countries, including the United States, the Soviet Union draws on a mystique—in this case, what it calls "Marxist-Leninist ideology"—by which it steers a course through such practical actions as detente.

Westerners like to be cynical about "true believers," even while venerating the Constitution, the Crown, or La Belle France—all of which have been altered drastically in practice over the past decades. They are comfortable with the assumption that contemporary Soviet leaders do not "really" mean what they say. There is truth in that assumption, but how much? Obviously, Lenin and his successors did not simply deduce detente from some body of received thought. But they did use doctrine to shape and give content to the policy, to

---

[16] USSR Mission to the United Nations, Press Release No. 55, July 2, 1974.

derive sanction for it, and to project expectations for the future. As leaders like Churchill, de Gaulle, Khrushchev, and others like them have taught the world, mystique in capable hands is a tool of policy that the adversary ignores at his peril. Five detentes with the Soviet Union have reinforced that lesson. It is embedded somewhere in every Soviet initiative and retreat, every negotiating session, every propaganda message, and it must be restudied if detente is to be adequately grasped and dealt with.

# 7

## Ideology and Negotiation

### The Ideology of Detente

Ideology may have ended in the modern world, as Daniel Bell and others have asserted for several years; but its hand, dead or alive, is still very much on the Soviet conception and management of detente. Marxist-Leninist theory has been milked, diluted, and distorted in Russia, as a host of critics from Trotsky to Mao have charged. What perseveres are habits of thinking unique to that compound of Russian emotion and German metaphysics, and three *senses* of what detente is to do, and why.

*The sense of threat.* "You are poor and abundant, mighty and impotent, Mother Russia," wrote the pre-Revolutionary poet Nekrasov. Both Lenin and Stalin quoted his words more than once. In 1918, while Lenin was at the height of Marxist internationalism, he proclaimed that "our unbreakable resolution (is) to achieve at any price that Russia cease to be a miserable and powerless country, that it become in the full sense of the word a powerful and rich country."[1] Stalin quoted the same passage in 1931, saying that everyone had found it profitable to beat Russia in the past—Mongol khans, Turkish beys, Swedish lords, British, French, Polish, Japanese exploiters. "Now we refuse to be beaten!"[2] he exclaimed. To negotiate with Stalin's Russia, Alexis Tolstoy told Ambassador Harriman during World War II, one must understand the Russia of Ivan the Terrible and Peter the Great. That is still necessary.

---

[1] Lenin, *Sochineniya*, 3d edition, vol. 22, p. 376.
[2] Stalin, *Leninism: Selected Writings*, p. 358.

The ancient Russian siege mentality resonated well with modern Communist class struggle. "The question is," Lenin wrote in 1906, "who will chase away whom or who will dissolve whom."[3] Fifteen years later, as the Soviet ruler, he laid down his classic dictum: "Either those who wanted to cause our destruction must perish—and in that case our Soviet republic will live—or the capitalists will live, and in that case the republic must perish."[4] No threat was exempt. When a typhus epidemic broke out in 1919, Lenin declared: "Either the lice triumph over socialism or socialism will triumph over the lice."[5] In 1929, Stalin said that "we are living according to Lenin's formula: 'Who will win? Shall we floor them, the capitalists . . . or will they floor us?' "[6]

Nathan Leites, who has studied Soviet political behavior closely, says: "The question of who (will destroy) whom is at all times the only realistic question in the relations between the Party and the rest of the world."[7] Former Ambassador George Kennan agrees: "The Russians have no conception of permanent friendly relations between states. For them, all foreigners are potential enemies."[8] Disarmament negotiator Arthur Dean found their "dogmatic expectation of hostility" from the outside world a formidable obstacle. Soviet behavior, he reported in 1966, seemed to "conceal a curious mixture of feelings of arrogance and fear."[9] Another long-time negotiatior, Philip Mosely, remarked on their "treasuring of grievances, real or imaginary."[10]

From the Who-Whom sense of threat, Soviet managers derive a number of assumptions about their negotiating adversary:

He is skilled and deceptive; beware his offers of concessions which, Leites advises, the Politburo cannot believe are being made except to catch the USSR off guard and to set it up for later blows.[11]

---

[3] Lenin, *Sochineniya*, 4th edition, vol. 10, p. 168.
[4] Lenin, *Selected Works*, vol. 9, p. 266.
[5] *Ibid.*, vol. 8, p. 72.
[6] Stalin, *op. cit.*, p. 100.
[7] Nathan Leites, *A Study of Bolshevism* (Glencoe, Ill.; 1953), p. 24.
[8] US Senate, Committee on Government Operations, Subcommittee on National Security and International Operations, *International Negotiation: The Soviet Approach* (1969), p. 4.
[9] *Ibid.*, p. 61.
[10] *Ibid.*, p. 77.
[11] Leites, *op. cit.*, p. 33.

He is rigid and unbending; dealing with him has only a limited chance of getting anywhere. Frederick Barghoorn has remarked that the Russian perception of their adversaries tends to be a mirror-image of themselves.

He cannot be compromised with over any length of time. The word "compromise" itself, as Mosely points out, has no standing in the Soviet vocabulary, and is generally used only in combination with the adjective "putrid."[12]

His morality is alien and hostile, so there can be no common ground on sin or expiation. "Our morality, "Lenin announced, "is deduced from the class struggle of the proletariat . . . (It) is that which serves to destroy the old exploiting society and to unite all the toilers around the proletariat."[13]

The sense of threat, obviously, is not absolute. If it were, no detente would be possible. But it is never out of Soviet consciousness, and probably never will be. A siege mentality is an integral part of the system of rule, one of the strongest rationales for the imposition of monolithic Party controls. Regardless of how warm any detente becomes, it is most doubtful that the sense of threat can be talked away or traded away by the United States. Who-Whom must be regarded as one of the *a priori* limits of detente. The task of the Soviet managers is to assure as far as possible that the "Who" role is not captured by the adversary, and "Whom" is not imposed on the USSR. Had these realities been better grasped by the American public and many of its leaders, much of the surprise and disappointments in this country could have been avoided, and the bargaining might have been more effective.

*The sense of rightness.* Like the sense of threat, the sense of being right is both old Russian and new Communist. In the preface to *A History of Russia,* Sir Bernard Pares remarks that "Russia, segregated early from Europe . . . developed a pride of her own without any evident justification except for the vague feeling of the capacities that were in her people, and this developed her distinctive-

---

12 US Senate Subcommittee, *op. cit.,* p. 21.
13 Lenin, Selected Works, vol. 9, p. 475.

ness and made a creed of it."[14] The creed "was strengthened by a parallel separation between the people, including the intellectuals, and the government. Both separations began much earlier and lasted far longer than comparable developments in the West. In Solzhenitsyn, they have come to the fore once again—to the considerable discomfiture of many of his Western admirers. While Solzhenitsyn finally broke with the Soviet system, it is also true that he lived and worked within it well into maturity. Thousands of other Solzhenitsyns continue to function within the Soviet order, finding less difficulty than he in reconciling ancient and modern totalitarianism.

Russian mystique and Marxist metaphysics have served each other well. In *Materialism and Empirio-Criticism*, Lenin laid claim to a superior insight when he asserted that "the sole 'property' of matter, with whose recognition philosophical materialism is bound up, is the property of *being an objective reality*, of existing outside the mind." Understanding that fact is what "distinguishes dialectical materialism from relativist agnosticism and idealism."[15] Marxism-Leninism is thus scientific because it perceives the source of truth and knows how to uncover it. Translated into practical terms, Lenin put the claim to the Soviet Congress in 1921 as follows:

> While we are immeasurably weaker than all other countries in economic, political, and miltary respects, we are at the same time stronger than they through the fact that we know and correctly assess all that issues and will issue from that imperialist confusion, from that bloody knot and those contradictions . . . in which these countries have entangled themselves, and entangle themselves ever more deeply, without seeing a way out.[16]

In a similar vein, Stalin wrote in 1934 that "it is a very rare thing for ruling parties to have a correct line and to be able to apply it."[17] His Communist Party, of course, did have such a line.

Convictions of righteousness, predictably, accompany fear complexes, and they are mutually reinforcing. No negotiator with any

---

[14] Bernard Pares, *A History of Russia* (New York: Alfred A. Knopf, 1944), Preface, p. viii.
[15] Lenin, *Selected Works*, vol. 11, p. 317.
[16] Lenin, *Sochineniya*, 3d edition, vol. 27, p. 115.
[17] Stalin, *op. cit.*, p. 359.

experience would waste any time in trying to win an argument with his Soviet counterpart. As British diplomat Sir William Hayter put it:

> The Russians are not to be persuaded by eloquence or convinced by reasonable arguments. They rely on what Stalin used to call the proper basis of international policy, the calculation of forces. So no case, however skillfully deployed, however clearly demonstrated as irrefutable, will move them from doing what they have previously decided to do; the only way of changing their purpose is to demonstrate that they have no advantageous alternative, that what they want to do is not possible.[18]

Every Soviet negotiator comes to his task with what Leites says is called *soznatelnost*—meaning, roughly, "consciousness." Consciousness flows directly from the "situation" and by the rules of scientific Marxism-Leninism, which alone can grasp the truth. *Soznatelnost* is an insulating shield which protects him from enemy efforts to sway him by playing on his spontaneity. Marxist-Leninist consciousness is not simply a mental grasp of concepts, but something that is part of Communist Man's very being.[19]

In a curious way, however, the sense of rightness also serves to mitigate the sense of fear, opening the way to retreat and postponement of total victory. "Strategy and politics prescribe the most despicable peace treaty," Lenin said of Brest-Litovsk in 1918.[20] "We must prepare ourselves for the possibility of retreat," he said in 1922.[21] Speaking of the Chinese Communist defeat in 1927, Stalin commented: "Only people who have broken with Marxism can demand that a correct policy should lead always and absolutely to an *immediate* victory over the enemy."[22] And in 1938, he said of Lenin's policy that "one had to know . . . how . . . to be the last to retreat."[23] The operative principle, to paraphrase one of Lenin's book titles, is this: "Since we are the sole possessors of the instruments of truth,

---

[18] US Senate Subcommittee, *op. cit.*, p. 29.
[19] Leites, *op. cit.*, p. 46.
[20] Lenin, *Selected Works*, vol. 7, p. 312.
[21] *Ibid.*, vol. 10, p. 323.
[22] Stalin, *Sochineniya*, vol. 9, p. 345
[23] Stalin, *History of the CPSU (B), Short Course*, p. 89.

we can afford to take a step backward in order to take two forward at a more opportune time."

Russia's detente partners are prone to see any retreat as a *de facto* abandonment of Soviet messianism. They underestimate the tenacity with which the Soviet leaders keep returning to goals which were supposedly lost in the onrush of "now" activity. Achievement-oriented cultures regard the "long view" as mostly rhetoric which, in the Soviet case, will have less and less meaning as detente engages the USSR and rechannels its energies. That may yet prove correct; but after five detentes, the basic time sense has stayed remarkably intact.

*The sense of time.* Time, or more accurately, timelessness, is the third dimension in the Soviet view of detente. It stems in part from more than a thousand years of Russian history and survival, in part from the Marxian world outlook. "We know that the transition from capitalism to socialism involves an extremely difficult struggle," Lenin said in 1918. "But we are prepared . . . to make a thousand attempts; and having made a thousand attempts, we shall go on to the next attempt."[24] Next year, he said again: "We shall act as we did in the Red Army; they may beat us a hundred times, but the hundred and first time we shall beat them all."[25] Explaining to the Comintern his offer of economic concessions under the first detente, in 1921, he said: "Concessions . . . mean paying tribute to capitalism. But we gain time, and gaining time means gaining everything."[26] Stalin was more forceful. Decrying the tendency to give up, he wrote in a 1924 letter: "The philosophy of *Weltschmerz* is not ours. Let those who are about to leave the historical scene and have lived their time feel distressed. Our philosophy has been rather neatly expressed by the American, Whitman: 'We live, our red blood is boiling with the fire of unexpended forces.' "[27]

These expressions are not mere rhetoric. They are the base lines for the Soviet organization of strategy and tactics in all its relations

---

[24] Lenin, *Collected Works*, vol. 23, p. 70.
[25] Lenin, *Selected Works*, vol. 8, p. 195.
[26] *Ibid.*, vol. 9, p. 239.
[27] Stalin, *Sochineniya*, vol. 6, p. 273.

with the outside world. Applied to detente, they are the rationale for a code of conduct which often seems inexplicable. Westerners understand the general distinctions between strategy and tactics, but the sharpness with which the distinctions are applied in Soviet practice is difficult to cope with. The difference between Western and Soviet conceptions of strategy and tactics is the difference in their sense of time. In 1924, Stalin laid down these definitions:

> Strategy deals with the main forces of the revolution and their reserves. It changes with the passing of the revolution from one stage to another, but remains essentially unchanged throughout a given stage . . . tactics pursue less important objectives, for the object of tactics is not the winning of the war as a whole, but the winning of some particular engagements or some particular battles.[28]

The 1963 edition of *Fundamentals of Marxism-Leninism*, a basic manual for all Communists, states: "The term tactics often implies a political line for a relatively short period of time determined by particular concrete conditions, whereas strategy refers to the line for a whole historical stage."[29]

One of those strategies "for a whole historical stage" is detente— or, to use its Communist name, "peaceful coexistence." "The Marxist-Leninists," said *Pravda* in 1953, "do not understand the policy of peaceful coexistence as a tactical maneuver designed for some limited span of time, but as the strategic line designed for the whole period of the transition from capitalism to socialism on a world scale."[30] The statement, coming at a time when the fifth detente was gathering momentum, can be read as reassurance to the Party faithful that their mission was not being foresaken. It also sets up a conceptual framework, which, in light of what followed, should be examined seriously.

Detente, as the statement says, is not timebound. It is not a tactic which is valid for only so long as it is required, thence to be dis-

---

[28] Stalin, *Problems of Leninism*, p. 84.
[29] *Fundamentals of Marxism-Leninism*, 2d edition (1963), p. 345.
[30] *Pravda*, December 6, 1973.

carded. Rather, it belongs with those "main forces of the revolution" that Stalin spoke of, and covers the "whole historical stage" set by the *Fundamentals*. It is, therefore, not of the order of "peace," as envisaged by the West, but of "peaceful coexistence," which is something far different. The *Statement of the 81 Communist and Workers Parties* of December 1960 spells this out unmistakably:

> The policy of peaceful coexistence is a policy of mobilization of the masses and launching vigorous action against the enemies of peace. Peaceful coexistence of states does not imply renunciation of the class struggle . . . The coexistence of states with different social systems is a form of class struggle between socialism and capitalism.[31]

Western leaders, especially America's newly-elected President John F. Kennedy, were far more interested in the "tactical" diminution of conflict that seemed to be implied than the "strategic" vows of enduring hostility that were plainly stated. They were soon disabused. In the years that followed, the two divergent time senses were never brought into symmetry. In 1974, as in 1960, and indeed in the 40 years before that, Soviet ideology continues to be a force in detente that must be reckoned with.

### Negotiation

For all its assumptions of superiority and certainty, ideology does not necessarily confer any insuperable advantage on the USSR in the uses of detente. Read by the United States without illusion or wishful thinking, ideology reveals Soviet vulnerabilities as well as strengths. Two systems of thought and action are in conflict, to be sure, and detente means different things to each side. But they are agreed on conducting the conflict under a *modus* that may be loosely described as "negotiation." Its ground rules have been forged in two generations of experience that has ranged from military confrontation to conference bargaining, enlisting government and nongovernment resources.

---

[31] *Statement of the 81 Communist and Workers Parties Meeting in Moscow*, p. 16.

American and other Western negotiators who have dealt with the Soviet Union during the five detentes are a reservoir of skills and insights for the tasks still ahead. Their advice and reflections form a consensus from which a working "how-to" can readily be distilled:

*Engage with prudence.* In accepting the 1973 Thayer Award at West Point, veteran diplomat Robert D. Murphy laid down the basic guidelines. After remarking that current Soviet efforts sought to use detente as a barrier to accommodation between the United States and the People's Republic of China, and as a way of acquiring much-needed economic help, Murphy said:

> We Americans should not reject such tactical maneuvering out of hand, but rather try at arm's length to exploit such periods to promote our own objectives. We should certainly use every opportunity to gain insight into Soviet planning and operations. What is important is that we do not confuse a tactical maneuver for a strategic change of Soviet policy. We should accept it for what it is—a temporary expedient.[32]

Murphy's contemporary, former Secretary of State Dean Acheson, counseled that negotiation for the Communists is "a method of warfare . . . dangerous and highly mobile adversary operations."[33] Leites warns that "the sheer power of 'negotiation' to reduce 'tension' " is a myth.[34] British Sovietologist Bernard Lewis suggests: "It may often be better to stand pat and do nothing rather than engage in activity. Action or mere activism (are not) always better than inaction in terms of both expedience and morality."[35]

*Negotiate from strength.* "As long as (the Soviet) system with its internal striving for power prevails," says Murphy, "and in the face of the huge Soviet military build-up, it would be an act of abysmal folly to relax our security efforts." Detente, he continues, need not and must not militate against the North Atlantic Alliance. Neither the isolationist nor the pacifist sentiments now on the rise should be al-

---

[32] *Assembly, Quarterly of the Association of Graduates,* United States Military Academy (June 1974), p. 30.
[33] US Senate Subcommittee, *op. cit.,* p. 28.
[34] Leites, *op. cit.,* p. 37.
[35] US Senate Subcommittee, *op. cit.,* p. 99.

lowed to cloud the true nature of the challenge.[36] Kennan writes that
the Russians understand the need to negotiate from strength most
clearly: "The technique of Russian diplomacy, like that of the Orient
in general, is concentrated on impressing an adversary with the ter-
rifying strength of Soviet power, while keeping him uncertain and
confused as to the exact channels and means of its application, and
thus inducing him to treat all Russian wishes and views with particular respect and consideration."[37]

*Be chary of the "agreement in principle."* We "must not allow
ourselves to be taken in," Arthur Dean cautions in words that have
special import now, "especially in matters of disarmament and arms
control, where we need extremely specific and detailed agreements
and verification controls."[38] If a statement of broad principles is required, says Mosely, "be sparing" in its use, and "remember that they
are not shared by the Soviet negotiator."[39]

*Stay clear of the "stacked agenda."* To the Soviet negotiator, Dean
holds, "the battle for the agenda is fundamental . . . because they
believe they can humiliate the other side and win or lose a conference
in this first battle."[40] Another experienced veteran, Kenneth Young,
cautions American negotiators not to be so eager to get down to details that they neglect their own starting platform. Too often, the
US team has suddenly found itself in a trap with no way out except
a clumsy "power play."[41] Mosely's advice is to "adopt a single clear
position, one which can be upheld logically and politically during
long discussions."[42]

*Know how to interpret and deal with Soviet rhetoric.* Longwinded
statements should not be taken too seriously, Fred Charles Iklé, now
US Arms Control Agency Director, contends. They are rarely intended to convey anything substantive. Nor should Soviet expressions
be allowed to infiltrate US semantics, such as "wars of national libera-

---

[36] *Assembly*, p. 30.
[37] US Senate Subcommittee, *op. cit.*, p. 4.
[38] *Ibid.*, p. 64.
[39] *Ibid.*, p. 25.
[40] *Ibid.*, p. 16.
[41] Kenneth T. Young, Negotiating With the Communists (New York: McGraw-Hill, 1968),
    p. 379.
[42] US Senate Subcommittee, *op. cit.*, p. 42.

tion" that liberate nobody, "Socialist" countries that are not Socialist at all, or "abnormal situations" like that in West Berlin which are abnormal only to the USSR.[43] One valuable aid, Mosely suggests, is for the Americans to have someone present who can follow the discussions in the original Russian without being handicapped by "the opaque veil of translation."[44]

*Be prepared for, but not intimidated by, acrimony.* "Do not be afraid of unpleasantness and public airing of differences" Kennan recommends. "The Russians don't mind scenes and scandals. If they discover that someone else does mind them and will go out of the way to avoid them, they will use this as a form of blackmail."[45] Communist arguments should not be assumed "immutable," Iklé says. All too often, US negotiators fail to put forth a point or stick to one because they think it is "unacceptable to the Communist side." In this way, the Americans actually make it so.[46]

*Know when to be patient, when to act.* "Strong but controlled feelings, rather than impatience or anger" are the only effective formula to start with, according to Mosely.[47] Kennan says: "If they know that their opponent means business, that the line of his patience is firmly established, and that he will not hesitate to take serious measures if this line is violated even in small ways, they will be careful and considerate."[48] The Russian will listen to his opponent's undertones, gauge their firmness, and the nuances will have a strong effect on his responses, Mosely asserts.[49] "Don't make fatuous gestures of good will," Kennan warns. These will only upset their calculations and throw them off balance. "Make no requests . . . unless we are prepared to make them feel our displeasure in a practical way in case the request is not granted."[50] But if it becomes plain that the Communists are not seriously interested in bargaining, that they have come only to make propaganda points, Young and Mosely say the best thing for the Americans to do is to break off the proceedings.

---

[43] *Ibid.*, p. 77.
[44] *Ibid.*, p. 497.
[45] *Ibid.*, p. 492.
[46] *Ibid.*, p. 74.
[47] *Ibid.*, p. 56.
[48] Leites, *op. cit.*, p. 57.
[49] US Senate Subcommittee, *op. cit.*, p. 58.
[50] *Ibid.*, p. 62.

*Stay with what is possible to get from the USSR.* Avoid pressing them for what you know they cannot give. Mosely points out that Soviet negotiators "even when under some pressure to reach agreement, have shown that they are in mortal terror of violating any part, minor or major, of their instructions, and are extremely reluctant to report to Moscow that they cannot get every point and every wording in their own drafts."[51] And above all, Kennan cautions, do not go over their heads to their superiors. That merely undercuts them with their own bureaucracy without producing any benefit to the United States. On the other hand, do not act "chummy" with them; they will not understand it, and their own people will suspect them of being soft on the opposition.[52]

*Negotiate quid pro quo.* This is Young's term, by which he means going for "clear, specific, and self-enforcing compromises which are reciprocal." The best bargain is one that does not depend on good faith, good intentions, or an elaborate and unwieldy machinery of supervision. Self-enforcing agreements are not always possible, of course, but they should be the model the US strives to follow.[53]

These nine injunctions for the management of detente do not, and cannot, cover all contingencies. Detente is still evolving, and what lies ahead is in good part unknowable. What they bring forward from the past is that the Russians, in the old cliche, are not ten feet tall. They have exploited the past and present detentes to good advantage; but for them, too, detente has its limits. They like to believe that "contradictions" are something that impede only the adversary. But they, too, have run afoul of their own lines just as often.

Something of a recognition of that fact shows through in the official Soviet *Diplomatic Dictionary*'s words. Diplomacy, it asserts, is a part of politics, and must therefore "be based on the conclusions of science. However, the application of these conclusions for changing the actual situation in the direction of determined political objectives is an art."[54] US detente management can safely agree about the "art,"

---

[51] *Ibid.*, p. 80.
[52] *Ibid.*, p. 77.
[53] *Ibid.*, pp. 35-36.
[54] *Ibid.*, p. 77.

leaving "science" in rhetorical command. Almost six decades of on-and-off detente with the USSR have perforce taught the American people and their leaders what it is all about. How those teachings are used in the unfinished business ahead, whether they are taken to heart or forgotten, will determine whether detente is to be an American art, or a tragedy.

**National Strategy Information Center, Inc.**

## STRATEGY PAPERS

Edited by Frank N. Trager and William Henderson
With the assistance of Dorothy E. Nicolosi

*Detente: Promises and Pitfalls* by Gerald L. Steibel, March 1975

*Oil, Politics, and Sea Power: The Indian Ocean Vortex* by Ian W. A. C. Adie, December 1974

*The Soviet Presence in Latin America* by James D. Theberge, June 1974

*The Horn of Africa* by J. Bowyer Bell, Jr., December 1973

*Research and Development and the Prospects for International Security* by Frederick Seitz and Rodney W. Nichols, December 1973

*Raw Material Supply in a Multipolar World* by Yuan-li Wu. October 1973

*The People's Liberation Army: Communist China's Armed Forces* by Angus M. Fraser, August 1973

*Nuclear Weapons and the Atlantic Alliance* by Wynfred Joshua, May 1973

*How to Think About Arms Control and Disarmament* by James E. Dougherty, May 1973

*The Military Indoctrination of Soviet Youth* by Leon Goure, January 1973

*The Asian Alliance: Japan and United States Policy* by Franz Michael and Gaston J. Sigur, October 1972

*Iran, The Arabian Peninsula, and the Indian Ocean* by R. M. Burrel and Alvin J. Cottrell, September 1972 (Out of print)

*Soviet Naval Power: Challenge for the 1970s* by Norman Polmar, April 1972. Revised edition, September 1974

*How Can We Negotiate with the Communists?* by Gerald L. Steibel, March 1972

*Soviet Political Warfare Techniques, Espionage and Propaganda in the 1970s* by Lyman B. Kirkpatrick, Jr., and Howland H. Sargeant, January 1972

*The Soviet Presence in the Eastern Mediterranean* by Lawrence L. Whetten, September 1971

*The Military* Un*balance*
*Is the U.S. Becoming a Second-Class Power?* June 1971

*The Future of South Vietnam* by Brigadier F. P. Serong, February 1971 (Out of print)

*Strategy and National Interests: Reflections for the Future* by Bernard Brodie, January 1971 (Out of print)

*The Mekong River: A Challenge in Peaceful Development for Southeast Asia* by Eugene R. Black, December 1970 (Out of print)

*Problems of Strategy in the Pacific and Indian Oceans* by George G. Thomson, October 1970

*Soviet Penetration into the Middle East* by Wynfred Joshua, July 1970. Revised edition, October 1971 (Out of print)

*Australian Security Policies and Problems* by Justus M. van der Kroef, May 1970 (Out of print)

*Detente: Dilemma or Disaster?* by Gerald L. Steibel, July 1969 (Out of print)

*The Prudent Case for Safeguard* by William R. Kintner, June 1969 (Out of print)

*Forthcoming*

*The Development of Strategic Weapons* by Norman Polmar

*Soviet Sources of Military Doctrine and Strategy* by William F. Scott


## AGENDA PAPERS


Edited by Frank N. Trager and William Henderson
With the assistance of Dorothy E. Nicolosi


*Can We Avert Economic Warfare in Raw Materials? US Agriculture as a Blue Chip* by William Schneider, July 1974


*Forthcoming*

*Arms Treaties with Moscow: Unequal Terms Unevenly Applied?* by Donald G. Brennan

*Toward a US Energy Policy* by Klaus Knorr

*Can We Avert Economic Warfare in Raw Materials? US Agriculture as a Blue Chip,* revised edition, by William Schneider